Point Break

AF729799

TIMECODES

A book series exploring individual movies minute by minute.

Series Editors

Nicholas Rombes, University of Detroit Mercy, USA

Nadine Boljkovac, University of Colorado, USA

Advisory Board

Paweł Frelik (University of Warsaw, Poland)

Andrew Gallix (Independent Scholar, France)

Colleen Kennedy-Karpat (Bilkent University, Turkey)

Scott Macaulay (*Filmmaker Magazine* co-founder, USA)

Shiva Moghanloo (Independent Scholar, Iran)

Björn Sonnenberg-Schrank (Heinrich Heine University Düsseldorf, Germany)

Steven Shaviro (Wayne State University, USA)

Constantine Verevis (Monash University, Australia)

Also in the Series:

Gerry: Movies Minute by Minute, by Nicholas Rombes

BlacKkKlansman: Movies Minute by Minute, by Alex Zamalin

Twin Peaks: The Return, Part 8: Movies Minute by Minute, by Jeff Wood

Neptune Frost: Movies Minute by Minute, by Steven Shaviro

Sisters: Movies Minute by Minute, by Johanna Isaacson

Point Break

Movies Minute by Minute

Stephen Lee Naish

BLOOMSBURY ACADEMIC
NEW YORK • LONDON • OXFORD • NEW DELHI • SYDNEY

BLOOMSBURY ACADEMIC
Bloomsbury Publishing Inc, 1359 Broadway, New York, NY 10018, USA
Bloomsbury Publishing Plc, 50 Bedford Square, London, WC1B 3DP, UK
Bloomsbury Publishing Ireland, 29 Earlsfort Terrace,
Dublin 2, D02 AY28, Ireland

BLOOMSBURY, BLOOMSBURY ACADEMIC and the Diana logo are trademarks of Bloomsbury Publishing Plc

First published in the United States of America 2026

Copyright © Stephen Lee Naish, 2026

For legal purposes the Acknowledgments on p. viii constitute an extension of this copyright page.

Cover design: Eleanor Rose
Cover illustration © Steve De La Mare

All rights reserved. No part of this publication may be: i) reproduced or transmitted in any form, electronic or mechanical, including photocopying, recording or by means of any information storage or retrieval system without prior permission in writing from the publishers; or ii) used or reproduced in any way for the training, development or operation of artificial intelligence (AI) technologies, including generative AI technologies. The rights holders expressly reserve this publication from the text and data mining exception as per Article 4(3) of the Digital Single Market Directive (EU) 2019/790.

Bloomsbury Publishing Inc does not have any control over, or responsibility for, any third-party websites referred to or in this book. All internet addresses given in this book were correct at the time of going to press. The author and publisher regret any inconvenience caused if addresses have changed or sites have ceased to exist, but can accept no responsibility for any such changes.

Library of Congress Cataloging-in-Publication Data
Names: Naish, Stephen Lee author
Title: Point break : movies minute by minute / Stephen Lee Naish.
Description: New York : Bloomsbury Academic, 2026. | Series: Timecodes | Includes bibliographical references and index.
Identifiers: LCCN 2026000750 | ISBN 9798216374152 hardback | ISBN 9798216374145 paperback | ISBN 9798216374176 pdf | ISBN 9798216374183 pub Subjects: LCSH: Point break (Motion picture : 1991) | LCGFT: Film criticism
Classification: LCC PN1997.P544 N35 2026
LC record available at https://lccn.loc.gov/2026000750

ISBN: HB: 979-8-2163-7415-2
PB: 979-8-2163-7414-5
ePDF: 979-8-2163-7417-6
eBook: 979-8-2163-7418-3

Series: Timecodes

Typeset by Deanta Global Publishing Services, Chennai, India
Printed and bound in the United States of America

For product safety related questions contact productsafety@bloomsbury.com.

To find out more about our authors and books visit www.bloomsbury.com and sign up for our newsletters.

CONTENTS

"In *Point Break: Movies Minute by Minute*, Stephen Lee Naish provides readers with a fresh and compelling model of how to experience movies—all movies—more deeply and with a richer, more nuanced engagement of intellect and emotion. The book is an elegantly written call to see popular cinema as an informative window into the complex, precarious, and confusing world we all share."

— Clarke Mackey, Emeritus Professor in Film and Media, Queen's University, Canada

PREFACE

Every minute of director Kathryn Bigelow's *Point Break* (1991) is a relentless thrill ride: loud guns, exquisite surfing scenes, a couple of brawls, a car chase, more loud guns, more surfing, some sex, a fast-paced foot chase, skydiving, even more surfing, and even more brawls. The film hurtles from one high-octane set piece to another at a breathless pace, offering what feels like a phantasmagoria of action and adrenaline—that is, until it does end. The credits roll and you leave the theater, eject the DVD, or watch your streaming service cue up a similar title. The rush is over. The heart rate returns to neutral. Nearly two hours have passed, yet it feels like only a few minutes.

Despite the abundance of slow-motion surfing sequences, everything about *Point Break*—from its whip-fast camera movements and rapid-fire editing to its punchy dialogue, high-energy performances, its synth-and-orchestral score, and rock-driven soundtrack—seems to conspire to keep the film moving at full throttle. Which is perhaps why there is such an appeal in slowing the film down and allowing each minute to take a slow, deep breath, and a long exhale, just for once.

This book, which is part of Bloomsbury's *Timecodes* series, offers a unique opportunity to experience each minute of *Point Break* as its own self-contained entity—detached from the moments before and after, yet still connected to the whole. It invites readers to explore the possibilities and peel back each 60-second component to uncover passages that suggest new stories or hint at fresh readings and understandings—whether within the film's narrative itself, in conversation with its surrounding cultural and political contexts, through the ways the film communicates with the past, present, and future, or on a more personal level. Can these passages create a new experience? Let us find out.

ACKNOWLEDGMENTS

My gratitude to Nick Rombes, Nadine Boljkovac, and the team at Bloomsbury for commissioning this book.

Love to mum, dad, Joanne, Libby, Evie, Kara, Gail, and Ross.

My love to Jamie, Hayden, Isla, and Puff the cat.

Immersion

Minutes 1–60

Minute 1

The opening credits of director Kathryn Bigelow's action film *Point Break* unfold in glorious slow motion: waves crash gently onto a golden, sunlit beach. The undulating layers of water glisten under the warm and hazy rays, creating an image that is both inviting and oddly abstract.

I love the water, but my experience with surfing is nonexistent, and I harbor no inclination to pursue the activity. Having not been born or raised near a significant body of water, particularly one as vast as the Pacific Ocean, I find the idea of hurling myself into the waves preposterous and perilous. Yet, I am also drawn to the rhythmic retreat of those waves. I want to step into the screen, feel the scorching sand beneath my feet, and cool them off in the vigorous surf.

A line from another film echoes in my mind as I watch the waves: Lt. Col. Kilgore (Robert Duvall) in Francis Ford Coppola's *Apocalypse Now* (1979) exclaiming to his squadron, "If I say it's safe to surf this beach, Captain, it's safe to surf this beach!" And indeed, I would try to surf this beach. It would be a disaster—but it looks far too lovely to dismiss the idea.

The accompanying score by American composer Mark Isham strikes a contrasting note against the bewitching visuals. Amid the powerful ocean swells and booming wind, an ominous, ethereal synth emerges, providing what film music critic Jonathan Broxton notes is "a deep, enveloping sound" that Isham himself goes on to describe as "almost like white noise . . . the soundscape of a surging wave."[1] The sound, along with the crashing booms of the waves, creates a sense of uneasiness for the audience, but also something deeply alluring: the "big booming orchestral chords capturing the might and power of the ocean, while the accompanying electronics give the same footage a magical, mystical quality."[2] The soundtrack hints that this idyllic moment is more complex than it initially appears—that something strange and sinister flows beneath the surface, drifting among the tangled currents.

Though there is little else, narratively speaking anyway, to compare, I am reminded of the opening credits of David Lynch's *Blue Velvet* (1986). The montage of white picket fences, happy schoolchildren, waving firefighters, and freshly cut lawns transitions into the scenes of crawling insects that lurk beneath this veneer of idyllic small-town Americana. The ocean's surface is pristine, warm, and inviting. But what lurks below? Can we ever truly know anything without peering beneath?

Text proclaiming this to be a "Kathryn Bigelow Film" sweeps across the screen, soon replaced by the names of the film's lead actors, Patrick Swayze (as the surfing guru Bodhi) and Keanu Reeves (as the hotshot FBI agent Johnny Utah), which drift in, merge together for a brief moment, and fade away as bold yet translucent block letters reveal the film's title.

Point Break was Bigelow's fourth film as director after the acclaimed *Blue Steel* (1990), *Near Dark* (1987), and her debut co-directed feature *The Loveless* (1981, with filmmaker Monty Montgomery), which featured Willem Dafoe in only his second acting role. Bigelow remains a fascinating director who has carved a unique role within mainstream action film—operating, as Sean Redmond describes, as an "outsider on the inside, subverting the machine from within."[3] Indeed, Bigelow emerged from the artistic world of the 1970s, originally producing abstract works of art before experimenting with film. Bigelow's prominence as one of only a handful of mainstream female directors, and one working predominantly in action cinema, is an astounding achievement.

Minute 2

The gentle tranquility is abruptly interrupted by a sound reminiscent of a gunshot, which is, in fact, the boom of a surfboard colliding with an incoming swell. A male surfer's muscular form sways across the waves in silhouette, framed against the low-hanging golden sun. He contorts his body gracefully over the water. In the midst of the disorienting ocean, the wetsuit-clad figure appears almost motionless, echoing the form of a Greek statue as he navigates the frothy waves in precise slow motion. With a swift turn, the surfer diverts the board away from the camera, sending a cascade of water splashing across the screen and initiating a cut to the next scene.

We remain soaked. But the once bright and carefree surf has been replaced by a dreary, relentless downpour. It seems we have shifted from the sunny climes of California to the damp locales of the Pacific Northwest. A young man with drenched jet-black hair, a tight black T-shirt, and seriously pumped-up biceps catches our attention. He casually pops a stick of gum into his mouth. Much like the surfer riding the waves, his movements are slow and deliberate. Despite his tough, stoic appearance, he remains unfazed by the heavy rain.

His expression conveys not danger or narcissism, but a quiet sense of authority. We are compelled to know and recognize this man's face, to understand that he is the hero of this story.

Of course, we the audience instantly recognize the face on screen as Keanu Reeves, at the time a familiar Canadian film and television actor whose comedic turn as the dim-witted Ted "Theodore" Logan in *Bill & Ted's Excellent Adventure* (1989), and as the stoner teenager Matt in Tim Hunter's *River's Edge* (1986), did not hint at the hunk of masculinity we find here. Nor did it predict the superstar status (and internet meme-generating fame) that Reeves would go on to achieve in the subsequent decades.

It is often noted by media critics, fans, and cinema audiences that Reeves tends to remain youthful in his appearance even as he, at the time of writing, has now reached the age of sixty. The face we see in *Point Break* is the same face we see in films such as *Johnny Mnemonic* (1995), *The Matrix* (1999), *The Day the Earth Stood Still* (2008), and *John Wick* (2014). The hairstyle might change, a beard might be grown for the role, but the eyes and facial features remain the same and still sprightly. Reeves's face is often the star attraction of any film he appears in. In Carmel Giarratana's essay "The Keanu Effect," she notes that in *Point Break*, "Bigelow consistently makes Keanu's face and body the constant object of the camera's movement," and when he is "not in the frame we momentarily lose interest, and so we are forced to search him out."[4]

This observation is noted when the camera cuts away from Reeves for a few moments and returns to the surfer whose face still remains obscured against the low sun. Presumably, it is Swayze, but it is hard to be certain, given the silhouette, the glare of the sun on the rippling water, and the lens flare that penetrates the camera lens. He remains an enigma. His surfboard swings and sways through the waves.

We flip back to the rainy locale. A whistle blows, and an FBI officer (played uncredited by Tom Sizemore) gestures toward the young man, who turns his head in response. Meanwhile, back on the waves, the surfer struggles against a massive swell, appearing less confident and more uneasy than before. The ocean seems to resist his intrusion. The surfer senses a shift in the tide—that his safety and his future are in danger from something unknown to him at this moment. The young man cocks his gun with a determined look, ready to take care of business. Shots ring out at moving paper targets in a gun range. They are cardboard caricatures of typical bad guys. As we alternate between our protagonist and the mysterious surfer, a contrast unfolds. The shooter is steady, calculated, and in control, while the surfer is at the mercy of the ocean currents, struggling to stay ahead and afloat. The shooter stands firm on the ground, rolls to take a perfect shot, while the surfer is tossed around by the waves. He loses control.

Minute 3

The gun show intensifies as shots ring out with increased urgency and volume. The synchronization between the rising surf and the soundtrack score is evident as the camera alternates between the two men conducting their activities. The pace of the edits quickens, creating a more disruptive, urgent, and unsettling effect on the viewer. *Point Break*'s editor, Howard Smith, is credited on screen just as the editing becomes particularly noticeable. As the gunshots subside, the FBI agent marks off checkboxes on his clipboard, raises his fist triumphantly, and exclaims amid the pouring rain, "100 percent, Utah! Good job." In response, our hero offers a wide grin and gives the other agent the thumbs-up.

We are uncertain at this point if "Utah" is his actual surname or some buccaneer moniker given to him by his team. Like "Maverick" or "Goose" from *Top Gun* (1986). It does not sound real. We are not on first-name terms with him yet.

The current state anthem of Utah remarks that "This Is the Place."[5] I suppose we could accept that this Utah we see on screen is the place/person we will come to know for the duration of the film—the hero we will now follow all the way to the end. However, the state's previous anthem, "Utah, We Love Thee," seems more appropriate to this situation. There is a definite, instantaneous infatuation from the viewer perspective.

Although only three minutes into the opening credits of *Point Break*, the contrasting characteristics of the two males on screen are already apparent to us. Utah is precise, composed, and efficient, achieving a perfect score on his assessment. His facial characteristics are observable. He seems relatable, a resolute officer in perfect control. On the other hand, the enigmatic surfer displays a more reckless and audacious approach while riding the waves. His persona is distinctly gung-ho. We do not know the face of the surfer.

The surfer vanishes beneath a cascade of water. The roaring surf melds into the noise of an airplane engine as it screeches down the steaming-hot tarmac of Los Angeles International Airport and taxis to a stop.

Minute 4

We cut to Utah, who is now dry, dressed in a drab gray suit, and hot from the stifling summer heat. He enters the offices of the FBI, Los Angeles Division, and announces his name as Johnny Utah to a receptionist. We now know his full name. Johnny—or John—conjures images of all-American cultural figures: John Wayne, John Ford, John F. Kennedy, Johnny Cash, as well as fictional comic book heroes such as Johnny Blaze and Johnny Storm. His name, according to Barry Keith Grant in his book *Shadows of Doubt*, creates "a mythic amalgam," in the mind of the audience, "at once evoking the American West and the western, as well as legendary athleticism in the masculine world of football."[6] The name recalls that of Joe Montana and Johnny Unitas (whom he will be mistaken for shortly).

Utah enters the maze of corridors, glass walls, and keycode-activated security doors where he meets with FBI Director Ben Harp (John C. McGinley). Harp is a working stiff, a straight shooter who does not believe in fun or recreation for himself or for his team of overworked federal agents. He does not allow them to drink alcohol or smoke cigarettes. His hair is flawless and unmoving from an ooze of Brylcreem. His suit is stiff. The highest compliment one could give him is that he "runs a tight ship."

The FBI office appears musty, hot as hell, and messy, with piles of paperwork stacked everywhere. It probably smells terrible from years of FBI agents' sweat and ancient cigarette smoke. The agents, in their wash-and-wear shirts, seem fatigued and grossly underpaid. The office, according to Tim Beasley-Murray in his essay "Play and Performance, Perfection and Pessimism: A Reassessment of (the Politics of) *Point Break*," is a "regulated domain of seriousness."[7] This "regulated domain" will eventually have to contend with Utah's desire for freedom and expression.

As Harp walks Utah through the office space, he (not Utah, who would be better qualified) fills in the blanks of Utah's exceptional education and background from his personal file, dismissing most of it as unimpressive compared with good, honest fieldwork.

There is much to a name, so let us take a moment to observe Harp's. Harp, as well as being a pleasant and often relaxing plucked string instrument, also means to nag, or, as the *Cambridge English Dictionary* states, to "complain about something many times in an annoying way."[8] To harp on and on. The name fits. Harp's only narrative function in *Point Break* is to continuously harp on.

Harp harps that Utah knows "nothing. In fact, you know less than nothing. If you knew that you knew nothing, then that would be something, but you don't." But Utah knows something vital to the position he has attained with the Bureau. Bank robberies have totaled "1,322 in L.A. County, up 26 percent from the year before."

Minute 5

"That's correct," remarks Harp in a confident manner that makes those dire statistics feel more like a boast of success than an admission of the department's failure. Maintaining the robbery statistics at a consistently elevated level keeps Harp and his team in business: no robberies, no robbery department—nothing for Harp to complain about. Despite Harp's hard-ass approach to his role, he is really a numbers wonk. His department uses "crunching data" and "data-based analysis" to attempt to solve these crimes. Beasley-Murray observes that the approach Harp and his team take is "bureaucracy and empirical science, with no space for the ludic dimension of freedom and intuition to which fictional detectives and policemen are so often given license. Utah, it is clear, is expected to learn how to perform a role that is less a role, in the theatrical sense of the word, and more a cog in a machine."[9]

While Utah chomps down on a donut for a full 22 seconds, Harp calls him out for being another "Blue flame special. Young, dumb, and full of cum" newcomer. He suspects Utah will be gone in a month or two, like all those other new recruits who have come and gone over the years. Some of them probably bailed due to Harp's persistent torrents of abuse. Others headed to cities where crimes actually get solved.

We have been on the move for a full two minutes within the confines of this stuffy office building. The environment from room to room is barely notable. These minutes only settle to allow Utah a moment to munch vigorously on his tasty-looking donut, which he does with a kind of dead-eyed detachment—an expression he will notably maintain for most of the film. The office feels oppressive. There is a desire to vacate, to return to those beautiful waves from only a few minutes ago. We feel anguish for what Sean Redmond refers to in his essay "All That Is Male Melts into Air," as Utah's "living death," noting that he "wants to be more than a working drone, that he will want to do more with his body."[10] The FBI is a place "without individual identity, without human embodiment, all technology, and no soul"[11] It is clear that Bigelow intends these spaces to appear unwelcoming on the screen. We want Utah to do more than sit behind a putrid desk for the rest of his life and crunch the data. In fact, we demand it of him. Our own visual pleasure and cognitive engagement is also of high importance.

Minute 6

We are back in the water. But this is not the gorgeous free surf seen in the film's opening sequence. It is an old-looking training pool situated on the lower level of the FBI offices, in which blindfolded agents are being timed to retrieve bricks from the deep end. This is a thankless task that means nothing to the agents or the work they do. It is clearly a sadistic event that Harp instigates as a ritual of humiliation. We meet an older special agent by the name of Angelo Pappas (Gary Busey). His name means "father" or "priest" in the Greek language. It is a fitting name. Though he is considered a leader of sorts, he is far from godly, but, from our knowledge of cop/buddy movies in which the young police officer is partnered with the seasoned veteran, he is rightly placed to become a fatherly figure to Utah. Beasley-Murray notes that "Pappas is something of a cinematic cliche: wise-cracking and hard-bitten, but kind-hearted. His clownish demeanor, open collar, and the Hawaiian shirts that he wears later in the film mark him out as a figure of fun."[12] He does appear a little older and wilder in comparison to the stiffly neat agents around him. He carries some extra weight around his gut (presumably from consuming the office donuts), seems less sharp, and is unable to take himself or his job too seriously. He has been in the field for twenty-two years. It is surprising he has yet to blow up at Harp.

Utah joins Pappas on the swim deck. They have been assigned to work together. Their meeting is tense. For a start, Pappas does not remove his blindfold. He feels the training assignment is an "indignity" to his years of service. He calls Utah (initially referring to him as Johnny Unitas, the former professional football quarterback), a "Blue Flamer," which the *Urban Dictionary* defines as a "new hire who is raring to go."[13] We get that impression from the few minutes we have spent with him. Unfortunately, Utah has been saddled with a department of number-crunchers and policy wonks who may not appreciate his enthusiasm for the job. Pappas finally welcomes him to the fold, and he tosses himself into the pool with a loud yelp.

Minute 7

We cut to the inside of a speeding car. A flash of images: loaded guns, smart dinner jackets and ties, grotesque rubber masks of former US presidents placed over heads. The masks bear the recognizable features of Lyndon B. Johnson, Richard Nixon, Jimmy Carter, and Ronald Reagan. These are the "Ex-Presidents," a gang of bank robbers who have been terrorizing the Malibu locals for several years. The detail is impressive. Chronologically, except for the omission of Gerald Ford, the gang are grotesque caricatures of the last four US presidents from the time in which *Point Break* was released in 1991. Reagan's former vice president George H. W. Bush was the current president at this point, having been sworn into office on January 20, 1989.

Perhaps because Gerald Ford was Nixon's vice president during the final year of his tumultuous second term, he becomes embroiled in that administration's failures and so gets integrated into the Nixon persona. After all, Ford pardoned Nixon for his role in the Watergate Scandal after taking office in 1974, declaring to the nation that "our long national nightmare is over,"[14] as he took the oath of office and fought to rid American politics of Nixon's stench. Ford's normal face does not transfer well enough to a caricature mask. I, for one, cannot recall his features without an internet image search, and I quickly forget his face within a few minutes after clicking off. Maybe Gerald Ford is too clean and therefore too boring. In his December 6, 1973, speech, Ford admitted as much by stating that his "addresses will never be as eloquent as Mr. Lincoln's."[15] He admitted the disadvantages of his drab personality too early. His one-term administration (1974–7) and the era it bridges cannot be so easily defined as Lyndon B. Johnson's (taking the progressive mantle from John F. Kennedy's popularity and rolling it into the "Great Society" project of domestic programs and legislation), Richard Nixon's (Watergate Scandal, meeting with Chairman Mao, the introduction of the Environmental Protection Agency), Jimmy Carter's (US energy crisis), and Ronald Reagan's (Iran–Contra affair, neoliberal policy shift). All Ford had during his presidency was a lousy economy, a swine-flu outbreak, and the ending of the Vietnam War, at a massive loss to America.

Despite purchasing the least expensive masks from a Malibu dollar store, the Ex-Presidents embody their namesakes' traits and personalities in a destabilizing manner for the bank patrons. It is an element that they all have a lot of fun with. Beasley-Murray notes that each member of the crew "performs his role to perfection, mimicking the voices and verbal quirks of the characters that they are playing, hitting the notes of comic and criminal timing."[16]

The Ex-Presidents burst into a busy bank, guns drawn and loaded, with plenty of shouting and marching orders. They immediately begin organizing the room. Reagan jumps on the bank teller's desk and proclaims to the captive patrons that "We've been screwing you for years, so a few more seconds (of your time) shouldn't matter." It is easy to imagine the horror of being a bank patron and seeing the mutated form of several men you may have voted for (or may not have) storming into the building and demanding not your vote but your money.

Minute 8

The Ex-Presidents are an efficient group of thieves. They know their remit and stick to it. The threats of violence seem real enough. They push and pull unruly or disobedient patrons to the ground. They point guns directly into the faces of people who freeze in fear. Yet, there is also a reassuring element to them: it will be all over soon. They take no hostages. Nobody will get hurt beyond a few bumps and scratches. Nixon is the one who truly relishes his persona. He communicates to the bank patrons and his fellow thieves with the same deep and pronounced tone of the real Richard Nixon's voice—the same voice that spoke to the nation in State of the Union addresses, or now perhaps better ingrained into pop culture today, impressionist Billy West's "Nixon" in the animated television show *Futurama*.

As the gang wrap up their robbery, having emptied the cash drawers and having not physically hurt anyone, Nixon raises both his hands in the air and gives the two-fingered peace sign that became a staple image of Nixon on the campaign trails and during public events. He proclaims to the room that "I'm not a crook." These infamous words echo throughout history, and it is important to note that the words spoken by the real Nixon after were "I've earned everything I've got."[17] Richard Nixon might have believed that about himself, but the Nixon of *Point Break* is not earning anything. He really is a crook.

Richard Nixon resigned the presidency on August 9, 1974, before the House of Representatives voted on articles of impeachment for his role in the Watergate Scandal, in which five men, working for the Committee to Re-Elect the President, broke into the Democratic National Headquarters at the Watergate Hotel and Office Building to photograph campaign documents and install wiretap devices in the telephones. Nixon's legacy was forever tarnished and associated with corruption.

LBJ, on the way out of the bank, drops his pants to reveal the words "Thank you" written across his buttocks. The words are too clear and precise to have been written by LBJ himself, which begs the question: which of the Ex-Presidents wrote the words on his bare bum for him?

We transition to the same image of LBJ's bum, playing out in fast-forward and rewind on a grainy surveillance screen, along with other surveillance footage of the crime. The footage is being viewed and discussed by Utah and Pappas. Sam Reimer points out in his essay "'Young Dum and Full of Cum': *Point Break*'s Homoerotic Haze in Five Acts" that the paused image of LBJ's posterior "resembles a man waiting for intercourse rather than a thief exiting a bank."[18] Indeed, as the scene shifts from the full-color image of the film to the grainy monochrome surveillance, the monitor "brightens the man's ass, illuminating the outline of his anus."[19] The surveillance image, minus the scrawled "Thank you," also evokes the graphic original cover art of rock band Type O Negative's second album, *The Origin of the Feces*, which was released the following year. The image features an extreme close-up of the band's vocalist Peter Steele's gaping anus.

Pappas recounts to Utah that the gang has robbed "27 banks in three years. In and out in 90 seconds."

Minute 9

'Pappas continues to tell Utah that the gang "control the room well." He explains the Ex-Presidents' bank robbery formula. They always stick to the teller draws, never waste time going for the vault, always leave a stolen switch-car running outside for the getaway vehicle, which they dump somewhere remote and then vanish "like a virgin on prom night," as Pappas colorfully puts it. One might assume that Pappas admires the Ex-Presidents' audacity. He even calls them "The best I've ever seen."

Two cocky young FBI agents named Babbit and Alvarez (Julian Reyes and Daniel Beer, respectively) appear and snatch the surveillance tapes out of the VCR player. Babbit mockingly asks Pappas if he has divulged his theory about the Ex-Presidents to Utah yet. Pappas looks embarrassed. "Hang ten, Pappas," Alvarez pipes up in a mockingly artificial Californian surfer-dude delivery. "Like totally rad, dude!" Utah looks confused, but really Alvarez is parodying the familiar SoCal vocal inflection that Reeves employed in his role as Ted in *Bill & Ted's Excellent Adventure*. Ted's full name in that film is Theodore, presumably named after President Theodore Roosevelt, himself an ex-president.

Minute 10

Harp intervenes between the four bickering agents with the newsflash that the Ex-Presidents' switch-car has been found abandoned on Mulholland Drive. Utah, ever the Blue Flamer, jumps on the opportunity to go and collect evidence. Pappas views the assignment as grunt work, the type of activity he left behind years ago. He reluctantly agrees to go along with Utah. Babbit and Alvarez gather the surveillance tapes and, with a few choice words toward Pappas ("what a hard-on"), head out. It is clear that Pappas is disrespected within the department. He does not do himself any favors. He is gruff, rude, and permanently annoyed.

By the time Utah and Pappas reach the abandoned car, it is late evening. The sky has darkened, and the vast, glowing sprawl of downtown Los Angeles spreads out toward the horizon. The illumination from buildings, homes, and cars twinkles and flickers like a quadrillion stars on a black-canvas sky. The real stars that would ordinarily light up the night are blocked out by the permanent layer of smog.

French philosopher Jean Baudrillard observed that there was nothing comparable to the beauty of seeing Los Angeles by night from up high. The city creates a glittering expanse of "luminous geometric, incandescent immensity, stretching as far as the eye can see."[20] This is the view of the city we witness here: alive and lit up, and offering variations of beauty and darkness simultaneously.

In his book *City of Quartz: Excavating the Future in Los Angeles*, urban theorist Mike Davis wrote that "Despite the mountain of gold that has been built downtown, Los Angeles remains vulnerable to the same explosive convergence of street anger, poverty, environmental crisis, and capital flight."[21] The riches that cities like Los Angeles hold within their interior are unimaginable, yet poverty exists, and means a gang of thugs in silly masks can hold up a bank every week for the small amounts of cash in the teller drawer and get away with it.

The United States government and state legislators, through taxation, will divvy up funding to police departments to investigate these crimes.

The distribution of wealth among the populace would make theft less probable, and the redistribution of resources toward education, creativity, community-based self-governance, and justice would mean less work for the police. But, according to Davis, "politicians reap greater rewards from lobbyists and conservative voters for building cells than for building classrooms."[22] This creates a self-perpetuating cycle of poverty and crime, leading to investigation and imprisonment.

Point Break is not an environmental film, though with its scenes of the ocean it does concern humanity's connection to nature in some capacity. It is not a film that makes direct commentary on climate change, which in the early 1990s was not a significant mainstream concern. There was knowledge that the air was getting dirtier (Pappas even makes that comment as he looks over the city from the high ridge), and the carbon output from fossil fuel extraction was depleting the ozone layer. The science of climate change was on the periphery and the real impacts were mostly relegated to far-off countries dealing with floods, droughts, fire, and famine. A carbon footprint was not widely discussed. "Take only pictures, leave only footprints" had not entered the public consciousness. Climate concerns, referred to then as global warming, lay in books like *The End of Nature* by Bill McKibben, which came out in 1989, and *Earth in the Balance: Ecology and the Human Spirit* by future vice president Al Gore, which came out a year after *Point Break*.

Yet, here on the high mountains that overlook urban Los Angeles, one cannot help but observe the smog and haze that impact visibility. It was notable in all the previous ten minutes of the film. The hazy sun under which the mysterious surfer negotiated the waves shone through a miasma of urban pollution. It not only hangs in the atmosphere but seeps into the FBI offices and the bank buildings. The people we have encountered so far all looked cooked from the intense heat. Everything appears hot to the touch.

Utah comments to a crime scene investigator taking samples inside the drop car that it is a vehicle without a built-in air-conditioning unit. "Yesterday was a scorcher," he notes. How can anyone drive anywhere in this heat without an AC unit churning out cool air? Especially after just robbing a bank in a three-piece suit and a rubber mask at midday and hightailing it away.

As the film progresses, environmental themes creep in around the edges, but for now, Pappas is hot and bothered about the time-wasting exercise of forensics. He would rather be anywhere else at 7:30 p.m.

Minute 11

Pappas's annoyance and lack of intrigue in the case ignites Utah's frustration, and he confronts him about the theory he has on the Ex-Presidents which everyone seems to mock. Utah at first taps into Pappas's twenty-two-year experience as an FBI agent but eventually discredits him as an "over-the-hill burnout" who should find a job as a "rent-a-cop" security guard and tell "Nam stories." This erupts Pappas into a rage. He grabs Utah by the collar and screams in his face about his time as a US soldier fighting in Khe Sanh during the Vietnam War. We understand that Pappas, like many veterans returning from conflict, carries with him the weight of post-traumatic stress disorder that is easily triggered. The Battle of Khe Sanh saw 274 American soldiers killed and 2,500 wounded.[23] Many of these men would have been comrades of Pappas. He possibly witnessed some horrendous actions performed by both sides of the conflict that stayed with him long after. Utah uses this knowledge to dig into the subconscious of Pappas and bring out the fighting spirit that has been buried for years.

Busey's casting is an interesting choice. It might be considered that the character of Pappas is a loose progression of his appearance as Leroy Smith in director John Milius's cult surfer film *Big Wednesday* (1979). Set between the turbulent years 1962 and 1974, and taking in the same Malibu locale as *Point Break*, the film follows Leroy, along with his friends Matt (Jan-Michael Vincent) and Jack (William Katt), as they navigate their carefree existence, their love of surfing, and the transition to adulthood in the shadow of the Vietnam War where they attempt to avoid conscription at any cost. When one of their friends is killed in Vietnam, the end of innocence and the carefree days of the 1960s is truly over for them. The three friends reunite in 1974 to surf The Great Swell and to reflect that their lives have been dramatically changed by the events and upheavals of the previous decade.

A sympathetic arc for Busey's Pappas could be that he was once an idealistic young man, much like Leroy, who went to fight in a war he did not understand and saw his friends and comrades killed and injured. He then drifted into police work and the FBI based on his record of service. The two films share several similar attributes other than a Busey performance. Both films reflect on the counterculture of the eras, the philosophy of the surf, and show some truly epic waves and surf scenes.

Minute 12

Pappas finally cracks and reveals that he believes the Ex-Presidents are a group of surfers. Surfers? Utah looks disappointed in this theory. What was he expecting?

This Mulholland Drive overlook of downtown Los Angeles and the San Fernando Valley is really the last we will see of any major urban landscape, for a while at least. Even when we do eventually return to the built-up environments, it will be mostly the suburban locations of Culver City. The film, from this point onwards, will predominantly take place along a wide stretch of the Pacific Coast Highway that encompasses the surf locales.

At exactly halfway through this minute, we cut back to the FBI office and to Pappas and Utah scrutinizing again the grainy, paused footage of LBJ's bare buttocks on the surveillance screen. Utah is chugging a bottle of beer, while Pappas takes swigs from a bottle of Jack Daniels whiskey as they work late into the evening. Pappas attempts to prove his surfer theory by pointing out the tan line across LBJ's backside. Though tan lines are hardly an uncommon trait in the sunny climes of California, he continues to explain that during a bank robbery the previous year, Nixon scuffed the counter and left a soil sample residue of "non-specific mud" that contained traces of Carnauba wax, which Pappas admits has "80-some uses."

Minute 13

Considering that he was the one who prompted Pappas to reveal his theory, Utah seems unimpressed and mocks his notion that the Ex-Presidents are a group of surfers, until Pappas brings out a can of Mr. Zog's Sex Wax, a common ingredient of which is Carnauba. Pappas explains that surfers use the wax to grease their boards, providing traction for the surfer while navigating the waves. Utah now seems intrigued although he still takes a dig at Pappas, asking if he is into "kinky shit." The slogan of Mr. Zog's Sex Wax is, after all, "The best for your stick," which one might tie to a masturbation innuendo. Utah only becomes sold on the idea once Pappas passes over the case file and notes that "It's strictly a summer job for these idiots." The Ex-Presidents have only been active from June to October in the previous years and Pappas notes that with one more month left of the summer season, "We won't see them till next summer."

It should be noted that this entire minute plays out with LBJ's bare bum mockingly looming between the two men in glitchy VHS on the surveillance screen, with a "Thank you" scrawled across the buttocks.

Minute 14

Utah finally gets it. "They're traveling on the money, going where the waves are," he states enthusiastically. With Utah's acknowledgment, Pappas deftly (for an old burnout, anyway) jumps on the desk and takes up a surfer stance, proclaiming that the Ex-Presidents "rip off banks to finance their endless summer." Utah joins him as they both scream "Whoa!" in a knowing parallel to Reeves's character in *Bill & Ted's Excellent Adventure*.

Pappas makes an interesting surfing reference when he mentions the Ex-President's "endless summer." Director Bruce Brown's documentary film *Endless Summer* (1966) chronicled the adventures of surfers Mike Hynson and Robert August as they traveled the globe in search of new breaks. Shot mostly on a 16-mm camera over the course of four months on a budget of $50,000, the film took in locations such as Senegal, South Africa, New Zealand, and Tahiti. For the fiftieth anniversary reissue, Ian Buckwater, writing in *NPR*, noted that *Endless Summer* was one of the first surfer films to introduce "surfing as the apotheosis of living-on-the-edge cool, with ripped dudes and lean ladies speaking a language all their own while devoting their days to the romantic pursuit of the perfect wave."[24] The documentary could be seen as a precursor to *Point Break*'s representation of surfing as something nomadic, spiritual, and cool.

This revelation that the Ex-Presidents rob banks to fuel their obsession with surfing is an interesting angle to explore further. In their book *Surfing and Social Theory*, Nick Ford and David Brown note that "within surf culture there are a (relatively small) number of surfers who derive a living from their subcultural or performance capital, notably including highly sponsored professional contest surfers, surf magazine proprietors and editors, surf journalists and photographers, the original (and thus in a sense authentic) surfboard shapers, surf fashion and equipment company owners."[25]

The Ex-Presidents, while made up of ace surfers, have not monetized their skills to make a living, nor have they opted to work within the periphery of surf culture—such as using the money they have stolen so far to open up a surfboard shop or create their own surfing brand. The gang might even consider the notion of making a living out of surfing a betrayal of the ideals they hold. Therefore, to continue to surf and live free, they have become common thieves.

We cut to a bright surf shop where a blonde fifteen-year-old male attendant (Christopher Pettiet) is selling Utah a new hot-pink surfboard. Because we have spent so much of the film so far in dark and dingy office spaces, in overcast exteriors, or at night, the shimmering pink of the surfboard ignites the screen with its brightness and stuns the eyes. The young lad finishes the purchase and signs off to Utah with, "Hope you stick with it. Surfing's the source . . . change your life . . . swear to God." Utah gives the boy a dismissive smirk. He currently believes that there are no answers to life's questions while sitting on a piece of foam/fiberglass at the lip of the ocean.

Pappas and Utah, both still in their suits, walk along the boardwalk. Utah carries the pink surfboard awkwardly under his arms. He asks Pappas why he cannot just carry the board around and "act stoned, ask a few questions." Pappas points out to the shoreline at a group of surfers bobbing closely in the shallows, waiting for the right wave to crack. "They're like some kind of tribe," Pappas remarks. "You have to get out there and learn the moves." Utah seems reluctant and questions, with some disbelief, "The FBI is going to pay me to learn to surf?" Pappas retorts, "It's either you or me out there on the board."

It is intriguing to note that the strange miasma of oppressive heat that has clung to the first 15 minutes of the film has dissipated. The color palette and brightness of the film have also changed. We are now in the bright, airy sunshine with wide camera shots that encompass the landscape around. There are no stiff suits being sweated into by overworked and overcooked FBI agents inside a hothouse office. The people who walk by Utah and Pappas on the boardwalk, or who stand by them casting fishing lines into the ocean, are all in bright clothing, tanned, and happy-looking. A gentle breeze caresses through the air, flicking Utah's fringe in different directions. The sky, rather than overcast or full of heat haze, is bright blue, crisp, and clear. Jackson Arn, writing in *The New Yorker*, notes that Bigelow and *Point Break*'s cinematographer Donald Peterman contaminate the first part of the film with a strange funk of "dull, grayish-blue interiors" and "grayish" hues that are swamped in a "*made of* L.A. smog" that then soon transition to a bright "yellowish" and further along the narrative a "cloudless blue."[26] This is a clever way for what might appear to be a police procedural/buddy film to suddenly switch gears toward the fun and kinetic action film we will inhabit for the duration.

Minute 15

We are 15 minutes into the film so far, and Bigelow has given us the framework from which she will continue to operate. *Point Break* is a high-octane action thriller. The scenes of gunfire, wet surfers, muscular frames, and the camera that glides and swoops through the action point at the territory we are in and toward the trajectory we will follow. Yvonne Tasker in her essay "Bigger Than Life" notes that "Bigelow's films have mobilised with increasing confidence the central qualities of action cinema—camera movement, carefully choreographed action, bursts of explosive spectacle, rapid editing—in combination with stylised lighting, careful composition and an urgent, sometimes erotic investment in objects and images: costume and uniform, blood and night skies."[27]

In the film's first 15 minutes, Bigelow's action filmmaking style is exemplified. She shows us small bursts of action that are tasters for the bigger action sequences that will come. Everything that Tasker notes has been included. Bigelow ensures there is no throwing us off the scent, no misguidance, no "rupture, spillage, or slippage,"[28] as Luke Collins notes in his essay "100% Pure Adrenaline: Gender and Generic Surface in *Point Break*" from the action-movie genre. On a surface level, the film glides along as an entertainment spectacle, but we are here to look a little deeper—and so is Utah.

Still on the boardwalk, Pappas gestures to the water and the surfers, and proclaims, "How hard can it be?" Without missing a beat, we cut to a towering and booming wave, engulfing a flailing Utah and swallowing him up in the white froth. The current drags him under once again, and he struggles to escape. When he finally pushes his head above water and catches a breath, another huge surge washes over and drags him under once again. From underneath the ocean surface, the swirling currents look like a series of raging storm clouds hovering overhead. Utah is tossed around in the violence, unable to resurface for more than a second or two before being swamped again by the cascading waters. The thrashing motion of Utah's body creates swirls of bubbles that wrap around his torso, as if they were ropes dragging him down.

In American writer Percival Everett's short story "Alluvial Deposits," the hydrologist, Robert Hawks, comments with some astonishment that there is never any new water on Earth. The same volumes exist and have existed for eons. The water takes on different states—liquid, vapor, and ice—and can remain in these states for decades or even centuries. In forms such as liquid and vapor, it can travel across land and traverse oceans. The same ancient molecules rise, fall, flow, freeze, and drain.[29] I think about this while I watch Utah roll and turn in these particular currents of water. The same water that is on screen throughout *Point Break* exists today somewhere, unlikely in the exact same location, and perhaps not in the same form. The molecules that form the bodies of water seen in *Point Break* have possibly been rendered on film before and after their capture here. Like any film that features a large or small amount of water on screen, here is a record of those molecules at a certain time and place—a snapshot before they disappear and reappear someplace else.

Minute 16

The raging surface water tumbles Utah over and sends him down into the calm depths of the ocean. He is surely done for. Suddenly, an unknown figure glides into view—a savior. An ethereal, twinkling synth fades in on the soundtrack as the figure pulls Utah from the depths, back to the surface, and guides him toward the shore. Utah coughs up a lungful of seawater as he emerges. This person—who we will soon learn is named Tyler Endicott (Lori Petty)—is calm and reassuring toward him. Even though we are now on the surface and no longer swallowed by the raging torrents, the two figures appear only in silhouette against the glistening sun and rippling water. They share a similar stature, their short hair falling in the same way. For a moment, it looks as if Utah has been rescued by himself. The comparison is also noted by Sean Redmond, who states: "One cannot initially tell who is doing the rescuing (man or woman) from the underwater shots (in fact it almost looks like there are two Utah's under water). When the two do emerge from the water their similar size, hair length, hair colour, and even their facial bone structures conjures up a doubling, a shrewd androgyny between them."[30]

Redmond continues that Utah and Tyler's likeness is "encoded through their masculine and feminine traits—they are both muscular, short-haired, but they are both pretty, 'soft,' fragile".[31]

As they make it to the beach, Utah collapses, gasping for air. His savior—now revealed to be a young female surfer—switches from reassuring lightness to sharp irritation, berating his lack of surf skills and mocking his "pig-board piece of shit" surfboard. A pig board, or pig-shaped board, is defined by Grant W. Kuhns in his book *On Surfing* as a "surfboard which is characterized by a narrow nose and broad tail"[32] and not particularly good for larger waves or fast maneuverability. She states that he has "no business whatsoever" being out on the waves. Tyler's entire rant unfolds while Utah, still off-screen, splutters loudly on the sand.

Minute 17

As Utah catches his breath on the sand, his savior returns to the surf. He shouts to her that his name is "Johnny Utah," to which she snaps back, "Who cares!" He watches her carve through the waves. The slow-motion arcs and whips of her movements recall the figure from the opening credits, but she is a more technically skilled and proficient surfer than the mysterious male seen in the dwindling sunlight a few minutes earlier.

We cut to our first clear look at Utah's savior as she changes by the side of her open-top Porsche. Utah, now dry and fully clothed, watches her from a distance through a pair of binoculars while leaning out of his car. The camera follows her movements as she pulls down her bikini bottoms and slides into her cut-off denim shorts. We are led to believe that we are viewing Tyler through the lens of Utah's voyeuristic gaze. A song by the California-based alternative rock band Concrete Blonde, titled "I Want You," bursts onto the soundtrack as the first instance of non-diegetic music in the film. We might envision that the song is playing in Utah's head as he watches her from afar. What does he "want" from her? Guidance on the surfboard, or something more intimate?

In his essay "*Point Break* and the Subversion of Surfing," Amos Lamb notes that the casting of Perry subverts the typical (up to this point, anyway) female casting in an action film. He remarks that "Tyler, an already androgynous name, doesn't fit the stereotypical mould of Action movie love interests. She serves initially as a mentor to Johnny Utah, a clever twist on the typical mentor/mentee relationship; her short hair and athletic build is a stark contrast to contemporary examples within the genre."[33]

If this were any other action film, the way the voyeuristic camera—Utah's ogling eye—watches Tyler undress might turn lecherous as more flesh is revealed. Bigelow resists this impulse. Tyler's undressing is filmed discreetly: clothing is removed, but no flesh is offered. Bigelow instead saves the erotic charge of semi-nudity for her male characters, who spend much of the film shirtless. Her interest lies not in objectifying women but in foregrounding the male body as the site of spectacle and desire.

Minute 18

Utah watches as Tyler finishes drying and changing, then hops into her car. He notes the license plate of her Porsche as she drives away. We cut back to the FBI office. Things are quieter, more relaxed this time. For a start, there is no Harp hovering over proceedings. The atmosphere seems less heated. Utah, no longer in his hot, stiff suit with slicked-back hair, wears a tight-fitting T-shirt, his hair less rigid. He is slowly morphing into the look—and the speech patterns—of a typical surfer.

The only one still heated is Pappas, who fumes that the contact Utah wishes to pursue just so happens to be "Female, blue eyes, black hair, five-foot-six, 199 pounds." "Not bad, Utah!" remarks the female FBI receptionist, Miss Deer (Sydney Walsh), who is helping Utah and Pappas identify the surfer. Utah reads the name from the computer screen, looming uncomfortably close to Miss Deer's ear and neck: "Tyler Ann Endicott, born 11-27-64." He then recites her past convictions: "Exhibition of speed. Indecent exposure inside a moving vehicle."

Tyler seems to have had a brush with a hedonistic past. Utah reads the list of misdemeanors aloud, not just to inform the room, but with a sense that he is reading a wish list of encounters and behaviors he wants to experience himself. This side of Utah will be gradually revealed over the course of the film: the boy from Ohio who falls in love with the ocean, who seeks out reckless action. But he is also searching for something else. A way to trigger Tyler, to pull her into his orbit. Much like he got Pappas to reveal his theory about the Ex-Presidents, Utah is always looking for an opening in one's psychology.

Minute 19

He finds an opening when he discovers that Tyler's parents were killed in 1984 in an airplane crash in San Diego. Interestingly, according to the National Transportation Safety Board, no fatal airline disaster was recorded that year in San Diego.[34] Perhaps it was a private light aircraft. Tyler would have been twenty at the time—not technically an orphan, but still old enough for the event to be profoundly traumatic. Utah recognizes this and knows exactly how to engage and subtly exploit it.

We cut to a dirty yellow-brown road, where Utah pulls up in his car outside a beachside surfer-and-biker hangout named Neptune's Net where Tyler works as a server. The air hangs thick and choking. To note once again, *Point Break* is not a film that addresses environmental concerns, but this brief glimpse of the choking exterior evokes the same heavy air that descended on North America in late June 2023, when smoke from forest fires burning across all provinces of Canada drifted across the continent, blanketing it in a haze of wood smoke. The sun shone through the smog as a bright orb and painted the surroundings in an eerie, orange-tinted haze. California experiences thousands of wildfires every year. According to the National Interagency Fire Center, in 1990, the year in which principal photography for *Point Break* took place, 66,481 fires were reported with 4,621,621 acres of land burned.[35] With that volume of fire, it is no wonder that the smoke drift would be evident in scenes within the film.

When Tyler notices Utah entering the restaurant, she asks him what he wants, to which he comically replies, "Shrimp and fries." Utah knows this is not what she means, and she frustratingly elaborates. Utah then states that he wants Tyler to teach him how to surf. She is unenthusiastic, telling him to stick to nice, middle-class sports like tennis or miniature golf.

What is interesting during this interaction is that the framing closely mirrors Minute 14 in which Utah purchases the surfboard from the teenage kid in the surf shop. Tyler is positioned behind the service counter, just as the kid was. In both scenes, Utah also stands stiffly in front of the counter. When the kid at the surf shop mocks his age, Utah defensively states, "I'm twenty-five." When Tyler asks what he wants, he responds, "Shrimp and fries." A rhyme appears in each response.

It is a small point that hints at something broader about Utah. Because of the narrative conventions of a typical action film, we are led to expect that Utah and Tyler will enter into a romantic relationship. It is also apparent that the sexual tension between the two must be defused early on. Back in Minute 14, as Utah and Pappas discuss the virtues of learning to surf, Utah comments that the activity is "for little rubber people who don't shave yet." In some respects—and this is not to disparage Reeves or his on-screen sexual appeal, which many find irresistible—we have to view Utah as almost a sexless entity: a "rubber person," like a Ken Doll or an Action Man, who completely lacks the apparatus for sexual engagement. With his almost unchanging facial expression, which Reeves maintains throughout nearly the entire film, it is easy to view Utah as almost doll-like. The reason for this dismissal of Utah's heterosexuality—or sexual allure—will soon become apparent: Tyler has a competitor for Utah's affections.

Minute 20

Utah insists that he will either learn to surf or break his neck. Tyler claims he is just delivering a flirtatious line. Perhaps a broken neck would be the better option. But then Utah solemnly reveals the real reason he wants to learn to surf.

> **Utah:** My whole life I've done things for other people. In high school, I played football because my old man expected me to. Then my parents always figured I'd go to law school. So, I did. Football scholarship. So, I'm a big hero to my folks, right? But two years ago, they were killed in a car wreck. You can't imagine it. Your whole life changes.

Except Tyler can imagine it because she has experienced it herself. The recognition of grief at losing her own parents is instantly reflected in her wide-eyed expression. The news about Utah's parents connects to her own loss. Perhaps she experienced a similar awakening after her parents passed, and the act of surfing became a form of therapy—one she knows can benefit him in his grieving process.

Minute 21

Tyler is drawn in, just as Utah had anticipated. She stares into his eyes as he continues his heartbreaking story. "I come out here from Ohio a month ago. I've never seen the ocean before. Any ocean. I never thought it would affect me so much. I'm drawn to it."

Utah is being dishonest about his love of the ocean, at least at this moment. So far, his only brush with the water has almost drowned him. Utah continues that he "wants to do what you do." He wants to learn to surf.

At this, Tyler laughs, but Utah's story has clearly worked as intended. She is taken in by his earnestness and naivety. She agrees to teach him to surf, or at least to show him the basics so he can learn the rest in his own time. She gives him one window of opportunity: 6 a.m. the next day.

We cut to the following morning. Tyler and Utah walk along the beach, silhouetted against the bright ocean waves, reminiscent of their first encounter.

We enter what might be considered a "classic training montage," in which a main character must learn to overcome obstacles and become proficient. Although this sequence hardly reaches the giddy heights of training montages seen in the *Rocky* franchise or *The Karate Kid* (1984), the same formula—intense concentration, uplifting music, and repeated mistakes and corrections—is present. Tyler begins her training session by having Utah continually jump from a prone position on his board to his feet. They do this on the beach, not in the water. The stride, posture, and balance must be mastered before even entering the ocean.

Minute 22

This repeated jumping and instruction draws the attention of some passers-by, who mock Utah for his lack of skill and his childlike ambition to surf. He ignores their mockery. Everyone must start somewhere; even the most seasoned surfer must learn balance.

Over the soundtrack comes the song "I Will Not Fall" by the San Francisco–based alt-rock band Wire Train. The lyric repeats the song's title over and over, which could be taken as a mantra of determination. Utah falls repeatedly but eventually begins to take on the stance of a true surfer, jumping onto the surfboard quickly and with ease. We transition from the beach to the ocean. Utah topples into the water several times, but manages to return to his board, regain his balance, and steady his posture. Tyler surfs alongside him, laughing at his repeated stumbles, but eventually dives off her own board into the water. Utah's clumsy approach to surfing, paired with his relentless optimism, is contagious. It seems just as much fun to fall into the water as it is to stand and ride the waves.

Minute 23

Tyler offers some words of encouragement: "You're doing all right, city boy!" It is clear from the fading light that they have been surfing all day. As they begin to wind down, they sit on their boards, talk, laugh, and flirtatiously flick water at each other. Utah takes another run at an incoming wave and manages to ride it until it fully crests. He is surfing—or at least he looks like he can manage a small swell.

It should be noted that this minute is a gorgeous tableau of Utah and Tyler, encased on all sides by the ocean. The waves flow fast in the foreground as clear ripples, while behind them, a blue, mountainous swell rises and falls. They rest in the middle, appearing to float in midair. In this moment, we are led to believe that there is nothing else of concern for either of them. Utah's original reasoning in wanting to learn to surf in order to infiltrate the community and uncover the identities of the Ex-Presidents seems to be forgotten as he finds peace and tranquility among the waves and in the presence of the free-spirited Tyler.

Minute 24

However, the peace and tranquility in Utah's mind is about to be broken. As he and Tyler exit the waves and return to the beach, the cheery music from Wire Train fades out, replaced by a strange, twinkling, and ominous synth. Utah's gaze is drawn to the towering waves, where a surfer—silhouetted against the low afternoon glow of the setting sun—rides the crest of a massive swell with expert precision. He is instantly mesmerized. Tyler, noticing Utah frozen in his tracks, sees it too. In fact, it seems she has witnessed this fanatical look on others before. "That's Bodhi," she states. "They call him 'the Bodhisattva.'" The name "Bodhisattva" refers to a "Buddhist deity who has attained the highest level of enlightenment, but who delays their entry into Paradise in order to help the earthbound."[36] This is a fitting moniker. As the narrative unfolds, Bodhi's relationships with his friends—and particularly with Utah—take on the quality of a spiritual guide, offering those around him wisdom and insight.

We cut back to Bodhi, and although his face remains obscured, we recognize his gonzo surf style and the familiar form upon the waves as that of the mysterious surfer from the opening scenes. Sam Raimer notes that this "tryptic structure" of "modified shot-reverse-shot editing" cuts between Utah, Bodhi, and Tyler creates a series of "unions and ruptures throughout."[37] Tyler positions herself between Utah's gaze and Bodhi's surfing prowess, but Utah pays her no attention. He looks right through her, mesmerized by another kind of beauty.

Instead of the low-tide, ankle-peeler waves that Tyler and Utah were using to learn how to surf, Bodhi weaves and straddles the monstrous swells further out in the depths. Utah cannot tear his eyes away. Time, for him as for us, seems to slow. Bodhi, just as in the opening scenes, navigates the waves in pristine slow motion.

"He's a modern savage," chuckles Tyler. "He's a real searcher." When Utah inquires about what Bodhi is searching for, she tells him that he is looking for the "ultimate ride!" Utah looks confused at this comment. What "ride" is she referring to? Utah cannot fathom, in his current frame of mind and limited understanding, what a "search" truly is. Tyler then comments that she believes Bodhi to be "crazier than you, Johnny." But Utah's "craziness" is just an act at this moment—a way to progress with the case.

As Bodhi exits the water, he looks back longingly at the waves he is leaving behind, as if his soul has been left out there, and the only way to reconnect is by returning to the ocean. Grant W. Kuhns observes the power the waves hold over a surfer and why it is significant.

> Man has, for centuries, been awed by the force displayed by ocean waves as they pound against the shore. At the same time, man cannot help being aware of his own comparative physical insignificance. The man who can match such a devastating power of nature with his own physical skill—and perhaps even humble the ocean with his poise and confidence—no longer seems insignificant by comparison.[38]

This is the ultimate ride that Tyler says Bodhi is searching for: an opportunity to be legendary, not just within the surf community, but beyond it as well—to be recognized and remembered in life and death.

As Bodhi exits the waves, a group of surfer dudes playing football on the nearby beach toss a ball toward him, which he catches effortlessly without losing grip of his surfboard.

Minute 25

As Utah and Tyler dry themselves off, a blurred figure emerges in the background, running up the beach toward Tyler while she towels her hair. The figure raises a finger to his lips in a "shushing" gesture directed at Utah, who glances over his shoulder as if the motion is meant for someone behind him. When we cut back, it becomes clear that it is Bodhi, running up to jump-scare Tyler. He greets her with an overly familiar kiss and makes a comment to Utah about his elaborate hot-pink surfboard. Utah does not respond. In fact, he does not acknowledge the comment at all; he simply stares at Bodhi in silent awe.

With his shaggy, shoulder-length bleached-blond locks, stubbly facial hair, and wild-eyed gaze, Bodhi fits the description of the "modern savage" bestowed upon him by Tyler. He is a man of distinctive and attractive features, yet they carry a slightly lived-in, untamed quality.

Bodhi takes Tyler aside and asks about Utah. Like a lovestruck teenager, Tyler fends off his probing questions. Off-screen, one of the surfers shouts, "Heads up!" as a football arches through the air toward them. Bodhi leaps for it, but it sails past him and lands in Utah's arms. Bodhi comments on the impressive catch, but Utah does not respond verbally. Having been all talk up to this point, he seems awestruck by Bodhi's presence and cannot yet summon words without sounding foolish. He takes up a football stance and tosses the ball back to the group of surfer dudes.

Utah's initial, wonderstruck reaction to Bodhi recalls another Patrick Swayze performance in Emile Ardolino's film *Dirty Dancing* (1987). In that film, Swayze plays Johnny Castle, a handsome and talented working-class dancer employed as a resort dance instructor in the Catskill Mountains. When he meets the young Frances "Baby" Houseman (Jennifer Grey) at the workers' after-party, she, like Utah, is momentarily stunned into a kind of dumbstruck awe by his beauty and presence. Frances watches in amazement as Johnny and his dance partner, Penny (Cynthia Rhodes), enter the workers' residence hall to cheers and greetings before moving to the dance floor with aplomb. When Frances is introduced to Johnny, she, unlike Utah, can at least manage a few words. She tells Johnny that she "carried a watermelon" to the party—a sentence she instantly regrets uttering.

Minute 26

Patrick Swayze is an interesting casting choice for the role of Bodhi. Initially, Swayze had been considered for the role of Utah, but with Reeves ultimately cast in that part at Bigelow's insistence, Swayze was instead given the role of Bodhi—arguably bringing the film more star power than Reeves could muster at this early stage of his career. Swayze had risen from roles in films such as *The Outsiders* (1983) and *Red Dawn* (1984) to becoming a major box office draw with leading parts in the aforementioned *Dirty Dancing*, *Road House* (1989), and the phenomenally successful *Ghost* (1990).

Swayze brings authenticity to *Point Break* in portraying Bodhi's athleticism and spiritual leanings. He had prior experience with surfing and skydiving, as well as an interest in Soka Gakkai Buddhism and Transcendental Meditation—practices that his character would have embraced, at least superficially. His characteristics as an actor, according to Brenton J. Malin in his book *American Masculinity Under*

Clinton, veered from "dangerously destructive on the one hand while keenly sensitive on the other."[39] These features made Swayze the definitive choice for Bodhi as both elements exist within the character.

"Ready! Set! Hut!"

It is night. The beach is illuminated by a flank of parked trucks, giving the scene the appearance of a small stadium. The surfer dudes, along with Utah and Tyler, are playing a game of football. If the rules of American Football (being British this is what this sport was referred to) were previously a mystery, the game being played here on the beach offers no insight into the rules and regulations of the game. One might assume that Bodhi and Utah are on opposing teams, but in reality, it is a chaotic free-for-all. The sand-drawn end zones are barely distinguishable from the rest of the pitch. How does anyone even know if they have scored? It hardly matters. The game is a masculine exhibition, with Tyler as the only female player, yet she is subjected to the same force and exuberance as the male players. As the game progresses, frustration appears on Bodhi's face as his team loses a point. Even in a casual game of beach football, he clearly does not like being on the losing side. When Utah receives the ball, he is brutally tackled to the ground by Bodhi, who snarls and yelps like a wild bear as he rises from the sand.

Minute 27

The game progresses. The score is unclear, the teams indistinguishable, and it is difficult to tell who is winning. We are mostly at a loss because the scene is situated in front of a series of blinding car headlights that obscure almost everything. Only the players' muscular forms are visible in silhouette against the lights. It is a wild ballet of bodies leaping, rolling, and colliding, their facial expressions muted.

One of the surfer dudes throws the ball to Bodhi, who appears far outside the play zone. He takes off—but where to? How large is the play area anyway? A few players attempt to tackle him, but he easily knocks them aside. Bodhi, with Utah now in hot pursuit, races down the length of the beach until he reaches the crashing shoreline. Utah catches up and barrel-rolls him into the waves. They are far from the pitch.

The cover of "Smoke on the Water" by the Detroit-based rock band Loudhouse, which has been soundtracking the play, suddenly scratches to a halt. An ominous low note rises alongside the crashing waves. Utah and Bodhi emerge drenched from the water, exchanging a tense gaze. Bodhi looks ready to lunge at Utah—his pride clearly wounded after being made to look a fool in front of his comrades. The other players rush over to confront Utah, but Bodhi quickly diffuses the situation. "Don't you know who this is?" he asks those gathered, "This is Johnny Utah. The Ohio State Buckeyes." Has Utah's cover been blown? His brief career as a football player before becoming an FBI agent has made him well-known among fans of the sport, even at the college level. Everyone seems pleased to meet him—they shake his hand and slap his shoulder, excusing their initial anger.

As the group walks out of the surf, Utah explains that a knee injury prevented him from continuing into the professional leagues. This is an interesting development. The story Utah shared with Tyler in the restaurant during Minute 20 may contain some element of truth. Threading reality into the false persona he is constructing is inherently risky, but it gives the impression that Utah is deliberately co-opting danger into his life.

Minute 28

Utah reveals that when his professional football career window closed, he chose to attend law school and now works as a lawyer. This news stuns the group of surfers. "Lawyers don't surf," says one of them, clearly bummed by the idea that someone in a suit and tie could pick up a surfboard and connect with the waves. But Bodhi seems amused and assures the group that this lawyer will surf. As they walk away to continue the game, Utah is left standing alone in the dark, illuminated only by the truck headlights. He looks toward them, relieved that his cover story is intact and that this community of surfers has accepted him.

We cut to a series of six CCTV monitors, each showing the same black-and-white image of Utah strolling into the FBI offices in his undercover surf attire: shorts, vest shirt, flip-flops, and a board tucked under his arm. He is also sporting an impressive suntan. Utah and Pappas have been called in for a humiliation hearing by Harp. In his office, Harp dresses them both down while other FBI members hover in the background, watching. Known for being uncompromising with his agents, Harp's voice escalates this time, his tone stern and overtly hostile toward both men.

From past cinematic encounters, we have seen enough of the "angry police chief" trope to know that Harp will tolerate only so much insolence before the gun or badge must be taken from the offending officers, or before the mayor breathes down his neck enough to warrant a dismissal. In recent years, this trope has been softened with the introduction of gentler, more understanding police chiefs. The trope was parodied to near exhaustion in John McTiernan's action-comedy *Last Action Hero* (1993), in which Lieutenant Dekker (Frank McRae) screams and rants at Detective Jack Slater (Arnold Schwarzenegger) to the point that his words become a series of unintelligible, unrelated sounds, with smoke emerging from his ears and head. Harp does not reach this level of absurd outrage, but he looks as if he is sweating napalm and ready to explode.

Minute 29

Harp continues his berating, informing the two agents that in the past two weeks of the undercover operation they have produced "exactly squat. Squat!" The final "squat," shouted with frustration, emerges more like a drill sergeant commanding his cadets to perform an exercise. For a moment, I am reminded of the formidable Gunnery Sergeant Hartman (R. Lee Ermey) in Stanley Kubrick's *Full Metal Jacket* (1987), berating his troops and repeatedly ordering them to perform push-ups.

Harp continues, "During which time, the Ex-Presidents have robbed two more banks!" Miss Deer nervously leans into the frame and closes the door behind Utah and Pappas. Once Harp calms himself, he asks if there are any further developments he needs to know about. Utah unwisely quips, in his zoned-out surfer speak, that he caught his "first tube this morning, sir."

We do not see or hear Harp's reaction to this comment but judging by Pappas's flustered mannerisms and his furious chewing of a lit cigar as they exit the room and move through the cramped corridors of the FBI offices, it was explosive. Pappas panics that Harp will throw them off the case if they do not produce some leads or potential suspects soon, but Utah seems unconcerned. He is chill. He has fully adopted the hazy persona of the surf dude and even drops a few surf slang terms into the conversation, correctly pointing out that the judgment to have him learn to surf was Pappas's "lame-o idea in the first place."

Utah and Pappas continue their walk through the offices, drawing bewildered looks from those they pass. Apparently, a buff guy in bright beach shorts, a sleeveless T-shirt, and a pink surfboard tucked under his arm is not a regular occurrence here. The office space still feels oppressive, made worse by Utah crashing his board into every corner and wall he passes. One could interpret the board smashing against the walls as an act of Utah's subconscious attempt to permanently break free from the FBI sweatbox and return to the wide, beautiful waves.

The two men enter the same office where they previously discovered Tyler's name and past misdemeanors. Utah, it turns out, has a lead: a hair sample from the Ex-Presidents' most recent bank robbery.

Minute 30

Utah runs an analysis revealing that the hair sample contains traces of selenium, titanium, and arsenic. He comments that pollution spills are always closing the beaches and that the territorial nature of surfers means they tend to stick to certain breaks regardless of water conditions. He then proposes that he and Pappas collect hair samples from beaches along the Malibu stretch of the Pacific Coast Highway to try to obtain a chemical trace match. Pappas hates the idea but agrees to do it anyway—partly to annoy Harp. The two partners share a spirited double high-five in true buddy movie fashion.

We cut to a polluted beach. Although a sign warns that it is closed to swimmers, the sand is still crowded with sunbathers and kids playing in the surf. In the distance, a massive industrial plant pumps out toxic smoke—the apparent source of the contamination. Two young men sit beneath a blanket, lazily passing a joint. Pappas, wearing a pair of ill-advised flowery flared pants and open-toed sandals, approaches them, flashes his FBI badge, and casually snips a chunk of hair from one of their heads. The pair look irritated by the intrusion but ultimately let it slide, relieved not to be hassled for possession.

Minute 31

Meanwhile, Utah is conducting his own investigation at another surf spot. He startles a young surfer by pretending there is a bug crawling into his ear, then abruptly yanks out a clump of hair under the guise of helping him.

We hear, for the first time, the full extent of the surfer-style speech that Utah has adopted to blend into the community. He drops "Brah" and "Bro" into nearly every sentence, punctuating his chatter with Beavis and Butt-Head-style chortles. His body language has shifted too. Gone is the stiffness of his FBI posture. His limbs now move loosely, his facial muscles slack, giving him a half-witted but blissfully content look. It verges on overkill. Yet the transformation is fleeting. As soon as he steps away from the surfer whose hair he just plucked, his composure returns, shoulders squared, expression taut once more. He can perform the facade of a stoned surfer, but it is not a permanent lifestyle choice—at least, not yet.

After the brief beach excursion, we return to the FBI offices—this time to a lab—where a forensic expert identifies a chemical trace match with Latigo Beach in Malibu. Utah, still speaking in his surfer speak—though here it comes off as more mocking in tone—remarks that the area has a "nice point break, long workable rides."

We cut to a muscular surfer gliding along the waves at Latigo Beach, confirming that Utah's judgment about the break was correct. The surfing here looks smooth and incredible. It is also an extremely popular destination. The beach is occupied by a group of territorial surfers who clearly view Utah's presence as an intrusion on their patch.

Minute 32

Utah moves among the surfers and is warned by one to "stay off my wave." Pappas watches from his car by the side of the road, binoculars in hand, while "7 and 7 Is" by the Los Angeles rock band Love plays on the radio. A swell begins to rise, and Utah paddles to meet it. The song transitions from the tinny car stereo to the film's main soundtrack as the wave gathers height and speed, the instrumental interlude of the song swelling in volume. Utah mounts the crest and manages to steady his posture, holding his balance for a relatively successful run.

Unfortunately, one of the surfers is already riding on it and heading straight into Utah's path. The two collide, causing both to wipe out. They are then engulfed by the crashing wave, and the surfboards are swept up in the white foam. Pappas continues to watch from the car window.

Minute 33

Utah emerges from the water slightly disoriented, but before he can even catch his breath, he is met with a fist to the face from the angry surfer, followed by a few choice words. A small knife flashes, and the surfer cuts the leash attaching the board to Utah's ankle, pushing it away with the confusing comment, "Politeness counts, asshole." As he paddles off, he hurls another insult, "Go back to the Valley, man!" In the confusion, we have still not had a clear look at the offended surfer, but the delivery of his lines feels oddly disembodied, like a non-player character (NPC) in a video game reacting when the player gets too close.

What Utah experiences is a rite of passage that all surfers must face to gain confidence on the waves—the so-called "surf rage." Ford and Brown note that this often occurs when "surfers are emotionally overtaken and resort to attempting to dominate the space, equipment, and even the bodies of other surfers, especially novitates, who inadvertently break the surfing etiquette on the waves and in doing so destroy the surfing space previously enjoyed by the individual in question."[40]

The novice Utah has inserted himself onto the surfers' turf, stealing a wave from beneath a seasoned local and encountering his first taste of surf rage.

Utah marches out of the waves to retrieve his board, which has washed up on the shore. He returns to his spot on the beach and makes a radio call to Pappas, offering an unsuccessful update. He then moves toward a covered area, out of Pappas's view.

Minute 34

There is a slow motion shot of Utah, still in his wetsuit, taking an outdoor shower. Four surf punks suddenly appear and menacingly surround him. They unhook the water faucet and the flow abruptly stops. Utah opens his eyes in confusion at the stoppage of water. The camera (which is point of view from Utah's perspective) pans from the first man, a muscular and mean looking guy who goes by the name of Warchild (Vincent Klyn), the second, by the name of Tone, who is instantly recognizable as Anthony Kiedis, singer with the Los Angeles rap/rock band Red Hot Chili Peppers, the third, a scrappy looking guy named Archbold (David Olson), and the fourth, the wronged surfer named Bunker (Chris Pedersen) from the previous minute. They all share the same style of hair, with long locks hanging over close-shaved sides.

Through decades of watching *Point Break*, I had convinced myself that the character of Archbold was played by Kiedis's bass-playing bandmate, Michael Balzary, better known as Flea. Only now, as I slow the film's relentless momentum and fail to spot Balzary's unmistakable gap-toothed grin, do I realize I have been mistaken all this time. Because Archbold is on screen for only a brief moment, and his face is obscured by wet hair, it is difficult to pin down his features with certainty.

I pause the film and click away from the screen where I am streaming it to double-check the Internet Movie Database (IMDb), making sure all the actors' names in this scene are correctly identified. Balzary, I discover, is nowhere to be found in the cast list. This sends me down a brief internet rabbit hole, wondering if IMDb—or even Wikipedia which I also check—might be wrong. Eventually, I skip ahead to the rolling end credits and, sure enough, David Olson is listed as playing Archbold. Could this have been a pseudonym Balzary used at the time? After all, Olson has only one other acting credit listed on IMDb. I begin trawling internet forums like Reddit and quickly discover that I am not alone in my long-held belief that Balzary was among the *Point Break* surf punks. Skipping Google's sometimes inefficient algorithms, I turn instead to the AI chatbot ChatGPT to ask directly whether Flea ever appeared in *Point Break*. It confidently—and incorrectly—tells me that Balzary played Roach, a member of Bodhi's crew. I correct the chatbot, and it concedes the error, though, in an effort to save face, it reminds me that Balzary did appear in a number of small film roles around the time of *Point Break*'s release. A quick scan of Flea's IMDb page reveals an impressive and eclectic filmography. He has had roles in the Bret Easton Ellis adaptation *Less Than Zero* (1987), a memorable turn as Needles in *Back to the Future Part II* (1989), and appeared in Gus Van Sant's *My Own Private Idaho* (1991), also alongside Reeves. His filmography continues right up to the present day. But *Point Break* is not among the titles.

I search for images of Balzary's arm tattoos and see that they differ from those on Olson's upper arm. Next, I look up images of "Flea RHCP long hair" and notice that the shaved undercut sported by Archbold in the film is not a look Balzary ever adopted. In fact, he has maintained either a short buzz cut or, occasionally, a fuzzy blonde afro for most of his career.

Slightly disappointed but also intrigued by my own small-scale Mandela Effect, I return to the film and continue watching the minute.

The surf punks close in around Utah. He attempts to defuse the situation with a self-deprecating remark: "This is where you tell me all about how locals rule and yuppie insects like me shouldn't be surfing." The gang, however, has other ideas. "That would be a waste of time," Tone replies coolly. "We're just gonna fuck you up," adds a smirking Warchild. The crew breaks into laughter.

Minute 35

With this unfortunate information, all Utah can muster is a deflated "Oh." Suddenly, he swings his board toward Bunker, then smashes it into Warchild's stomach—who, with almost effortless strength, snaps it clean in half. Goodbye, pink pig board. Utah lands a swift punch that sends Tone sprawling to the sand. Archbold connects with a jab to Utah's side, while Warchild delivers several brutal kicks to his torso, knocking him down. Tone charges again but is tossed aside with ease. Warchild then wraps a surf leash around Utah's neck as the others take turns pounding his gut. Meanwhile, Pappas—still sitting in the car, unaware of what's unfolding—tries to reach Utah on the radio.

Suddenly, Bunker is yanked to the ground by a pair of hands. It is Bodhi—arriving just in time to pull Utah out of the ruckus. He orders Warchild, who is still choking Utah, to "Back off. Seriously." When Warchild finally releases Utah, Bodhi follows with an oddly courteous "Thank you." Politeness, it seems, really does count when dealing with these surf punks. The phrase, of course, echoes the words scrawled across LBJ's backside during the first bank robbery—an image that later lingered on the FBI surveillance monitors as Utah and Pappas studied the Ex-Presidents' tactics. Here, the line's reappearance feels like more than a throwaway bit of irony. Could this be an early, subtle hint toward Bodhi's true identity?

Although Utah is positioned as the film's hero, it is worth noting how frequently he requires rescue. Left to his own devices, he gets into trouble and depends on others to pull him out. In Minute 16, it is Tyler who saves him from drowning, establishing her as both caretaker and gatekeeper to the surf world. Here, Bodhi intervenes to save him from a brutal beating, taking on the role of a protector. Later in the film, Pappas will drag Utah out of a crisis of his own making. Each rescue underscores Utah's reliance on others and subtly inverts the expected traits of the cinematic hero—he is the one who must be saved before he can save anyone else. As Katherine Barscay notes in her essay "Kathryn Bigelow's Gen(d)re," Utah becomes at numerous times during the film a "damsel-in-distress figure."[41] He often needs someone wiser, stronger, or older to pull him from danger. His competency, at best, is below average. In a more traditional action film, the male hero would rely on no one—using only his cunning and brutality to deliver swift justice, often punctuated by a quippy one-liner as he dispatches his enemies. Utah, however, continually stumbles, falters, and depends on others for survival. This marks yet another of Bigelow's subversive turns within the action genre—she takes the familiar macho framework and quietly undermines it from within.

Catching his breath, Utah says he is glad the surf punks found him.

Minute 36

When Bunker sarcastically asks why that is, Utah responds with a punch to his face. Tone tries to intervene but is quickly tossed back to the ground by Bodhi. Pappas, seeing the commotion from the road, runs to assist—but he is hardly needed. Bodhi and Utah handle the surf punks with ease, flooring them with a series of precise kicks and chops.

"This is stimulating, but we're outta here," Bodhi says as they leave the gang groaning on the sand, clutching their various injuries. The two men begin climbing a set of steps leading to the highway when Pappas suddenly appears, huffing and flushed from exertion. To justify his appearance, he concocts a story about a kid stealing his car stereo. Utah, unconcerned, tells him to go check on the four bleeding surf punks still sprawled on the beach.

Minute 37

There has been little room to take a breath during the first 35 minutes of the film. A sense of relentless acceleration has been prominent as the narrative sets Utah quickly on the path of surfing and infiltration. So far, the film has been drenched in fast-paced editing, fluid camera movements, surfing montages, near drownings, bank robberies, fights, and a barrage of loud conversations—mostly emanating from Harp. Minute 37 offers a rare moment for reflection, captured in a single, unbroken shot of Utah and Bodhi walking and talking as the adrenaline from their fight dissipates. A gentle, rising orchestral note quivers on the soundtrack beneath their dialogue.

In an interview with Gavin Smith for *Film Comment*, Bigelow stated that this scene was one of many "rest notes" found among the velocity of the film. Bigelow comments that "You need rest moments where the camera is simply covering two people in an unbroken wide shot, and you see the body language. It's a cinematic exhale."[42]

We feel this "cinematic exhale" as an audience, but it also offers the two characters on screen an opportunity to pause, reflect, and engage with one another. This is really the first time that Utah has had Bodhi just to himself. The two walk and talk side by side. The body language is reflected in each stride.

Utah asks about Warchild and his posse, asking who they are and what their agenda might be. "Nazi assholes," Bodhi confidently replies. "They think they're some kind of death squad around here." Utah casually probes further, asking if Bodhi knows about any illegal activities the group might be involved in. Bodhi shrugs: he does not care to answer and does not know enough to speculate. His concern lies elsewhere: Warchild and his gang are spiritually disconnected from the surfer lifestyle and have failed to attune themselves to the ocean. "They only live to get radical. They don't have any real understanding of the seas so they'll never get the spiritual side of it," he states. Utah jokes, "Hey, you're not going to start chanting, or anything, are you?" Bodhi laughs and offers a slice of his philosophy: surfing, he says, is "a state of mind. It's that place where you lose yourself and you find yourself."

In an essay included in *Point Break: Surfers and Waves*, a collection of American artist Raymond Pettibon's paintings and drawings of surfers and their environs, art historian Brian Lukacher eloquently observes that surfing is about "Submersion and levitation; disintegration and purification; terrifying loss of physical control and unexpected triumph of bodily composure within the most violent of natural forces."[43] A condition of losing yourself (your control, your responsibilities) and finding yourself (your composure, your fearlessness).

Although we, the audience, suspect (or maybe "expect") Bodhi to be the ringleader of the Ex-Presidents, it is not surprising that Utah does not at this point. Based on the terrifying violence of the bank robberies he has witnessed on the surveillance screens, Bodhi's spiritual calm, intelligence, and altruism do not fit the profile of a sadistic bank robber who likes to dress up as a former US president, point guns in people's faces, and scream orders at them. At this point, Utah is more focused on Warchild's gang of surf punks, who seem a better fit for the Ex-Presidents' violent profile.

Minute 38

As Utah reaches his car, he thanks Bodhi for stepping into the fight. Bodhi responds, "De nada" (meaning "you're welcome" in Spanish), and the two men shake hands. As he leaves, Bodhi turns to Utah and invites him to a party at his house later in the evening, directing him to bring Tyler along.

While *Point Break* is not a direct adaptation of Ken Nunn's 1984 novel *Tapping the Source*, it shares thematic elements and character similarities that invite comparison. Both works feature idyllic California beach locations. The book's young protagonist, Ike Tucker, like Utah, infiltrates a group of territorial surfers to find clues to his sister's disappearance. Once accepted, Tucker falls into the orbit of the charismatic surfer Hound Adams, who, like Bodhi, combines anti-establishment inclinations with a dark, criminal side. In *Tapping the Source*, the characters surf not merely for sport but for a metaphysical and spiritual pursuit that offers transcendence. Bodhi and his crew share a similar stance, seeking to break out of normative lifestyles and find tranquility among the waves.

The relative calm we just witnessed is interrupted when Pappas launches a Harp impersonation at Utah for moving out of sight during the fight. The two agents are now in hot pursuit of Warchild and his gang, who weave dangerously through freeway traffic in an old jeep, verbally abusing other drivers.

Utah contacts Miss Deer back at FBI headquarters over the police radio and asks for a run of the jeep's plates. As they enter a rundown suburban neighborhood and the jeep pulls into a shady-looking house, Utah receives the factsheet on Bunker Weiss, the jeep's owner, and the surfer he wronged. "The guy's got quite a sheet: felony possession of cocaine, felony B&E (breaking and entering), three months in juvie, felony assault. These guys really fit the profile."

Minute 39

We are on the same street, but it is now nighttime. Utah and Pappas are stationed outside the surf punks' house while a rowdy party is happening inside. Babbit and Alvarez pull up in their car to take on overnight surveillance of the house. They are both displeased with the assignment, but Alvarez is the most vocal. Pappas offers them some cold pizza as a consolation. Babbit winds up a middle finger toward them as they drive off. Pappas informs Utah that a warrant to search the house will be issued first thing in the morning by Harp and that he should return home to "get some sleep." But Utah has a house party to attend.

Jimi Hendrix's "If 6 Was 9" intrudes upon the soundtrack with its stabbing, distorted electric guitar. It arrives just as abruptly as it does in director Dennis Hopper's counterculture classic *Easy Rider* (1969), when the two hippie bikers, Billy and Wyatt (Dennis Hopper and Peter Fonda, respectively), who have traveled across the wide-open countryside to the gentle waves of psychedelic folk music in the first part of the film, suddenly enter the urban cityscape and the film takes a darker turn. The song's use here is an interesting connection, signifying a bridge between one counterculture—the radicals, hippies, and drug users of the 1960s—and another that represents surfing, extreme sports, and blissful natural adrenaline highs. Both lifestyles embody an anti-establishment and anti-materialist stance. But *Easy Rider*'s apparent idealism is a false flag, as noted by Lee Hill, "it is intriguing that many viewers and critics recall the film as an artifact of 60s idealism rather than as a harbinger of the increasingly cynical tone of the decades to come."[44] That cynicism is somewhat embodied by *Point Break*'s spiritual surfers who also rob banks while dressed in the disguises of former US presidents, whose policies and ideologies failed to allow the spirit of the 1960s to flourish in the following decades.

The Ex-Presidents share a similar understanding with Billy and Wyatt: society cannot be fixed through altruism, only through selfish endeavors. Billy and Wyatt score a major drug deal in Mexico and ride off to drop out of society, while the Ex-Presidents steal to satisfy their own desires and live a life off the grid.

Surfing's idealist nature in the 1960s offered, according to Mark Stranger in his book *Surfing Life: Surface, Substructure and the Commodification of the Sublime*, a "natural affiliation with the Dionysian ethos of the 1960s counter culture movement meant that even those oriented to surfing as an organized sport were affected. Drugs, sexual freedom, and dropping out became synonymous with a now even more oppositional subculture."[45]

This countercultural idealism also connects to the era in which *Point Break* was made. The surfing and extreme sports premise signaled an interest in adrenaline-fueled sports and alternative, nonconformist lifestyles that were prevalent at the time—a desire to be free, disconnect from "the system," and stick it to "the Man." Here was an echo of the 1960s counterculture, but instead of flared pants, it was swim shorts and tan lines. Like the Boomers before them, Generation Xers were poised to rebel against a decade of Ronald Reagan's government of "squares," which reverted to 1950s-style American jingoism, moral family values, and economic expansionism. By employing recycled terminology from sixties phrases such as "man," "cool," and "radical" (or "rad"), young people in the early 1990s—especially surfers—were taking cues from the progressive movements of the 1960s, but, like Billy and Wyatt, funneling them through individualistic perspectives and outcomes.

Much like the psychedelic rock of Jimi Hendrix and the protest folk music of Bob Dylan that soundtracked the cultural shift of the 1960s, the early 1990s had its own form of music that spoke of rebellion and disconnection from so-called mainstream society. Punk rock fused with melancholia, and a "heart-on-sleeve" lyricism brought grunge music to the surface as a deliberate reaction to the slick polish of 1980s hair metal bands like Mötley Crüe and Warrant, 1980s soft rock soul like Phil Collins and Michael Bolton, and bubblegum pop music such as Madonna and Tiffany. While they maintained the long hair, the grunge bands did not use hair products, wear makeup or spandex trousers. Instead, they wore plaid shirts, ripped jeans, cut-off shorts, drank too much coffee, smoked too much dope, talked openly about politics, watched dumb movies, were addicted to MTV, and, importantly, surfed, or skateboarded. The surfers and grungers were the disillusioned hippies of the 1990s, but with added cynicism and humor.

We enter Bodhi's abode and the gathering is lively. In comparison to the snippets of the party we saw happening across town at the surf punks' house, this one is far more pleasant and inclusive. A female partygoer blows a great blaze of flame across the screen from a lit torch, and the crowd goes wild.

Minute 40

Utah and Tyler move through the party, and the camera observes the patrons dancing and performing for it. We assume the viewpoint is from Utah's own eyes. The camera settles on one patron who performs a sudden seizure as if he were throwing up. We then come across one of Bodhi's friends from the football game mixing dancing with what looks like a form of Tai chi. It is an oddball party, but, as Sam Raimer notes, a harmless representation of "token sub-cultures of the early 1990s."[46]

The camera pulls toward a young woman dancing seductively, her hand movements guiding the camera's eye toward Bodhi. He is in the embrace of another female partygoer, nibbling candies from her necklace. He acknowledges Utah, then takes a shot of tequila, followed by sucking a lime held in his partner's teeth. Utah watches the interaction with the unimpressed and maddened expression of a scorned lover. Tyler, also unimpressed, informs the woman that she "taught him that trick." Bodhi says to Utah, with a slight nod toward Tyler but also acknowledging his own detachment from materialism, "Make yourself at home. What's mine is yours." It appears Bodhi is giving Utah permission to court Tyler. This, according to Yvonne Tasker in her book *Spectacular Bodies*, places Tyler in the position of a "token object of exchange" between "the two men's struggle with each other."[47] This could be considered a power play on Bodhi's part, a way to draw Utah further into the fold by encouraging his pursuit of Tyler.

Tyler pulls Utah away from Bodhi's orbit. He follows reluctantly, casting a longing glance back as he goes.

We move to the outside of Bodhi's house. It is a little later in the evening. A group of partygoers sits around a firepit, drinking beer and sharing surf stories.

Minute 41

Around the firepit, we are properly introduced to the rest of Bodhi's friends, starting with Grommet (Bojesse Christopher), who, with his long blonde hair, perpetually stoned expression, and "rad" speech style, is the most surfer-like of the four friends. He is also clearly the youngest of the group. As Grommet raps about a huge ocean swell he once conquered, Nathaniel (John Philbin) shakes a bottle of beer and sprays it in his direction, imitating the spray of the surf. Nathaniel appears slightly older and sports a thin mustache and chin beard. Roach (James Le Gros) then interjects with a comment about how lethal a wave can be if not approached correctly. Tyler interrupts the masculine direction of the conversation with a comment about how "Big-wave riding is for macho assholes with a death wish." Roach takes offense and tells the group that the sensation is "better than sex." Tyler deflates this by suggesting that Roach is not having sexual intercourse correctly.

There is no doubt that riding the big waves is Bodhi and his crew's main draw. After all, they are often out to prove their masculinity to themselves and to others. According to Nick Ford and David Brown, to negotiate the big waves, surfers need to ultimately

> be very strong, fit, technically skilled and heroically brave to pit themselves against the forces of nature. In terms of the gender order, the return to the heroic masculinities of the early days of surfing is no coincidence, it is the carving out of new territory and establishing new distance between the hegemonic masculine male surfer and the "Other" (i.e. all females and all the other men).[48]

Bodhi and the crew's desire is to survive the big waves and return victorious to prestige and celebration. If not, then to die valiantly trying, and leave a particular break or surf contest named in honor of their sacrifice, living on forever in notoriety.

Utah is hooked into the conversation and asks the group about the biggest surfs they have encountered. Nathaniel chooses Makaha, Hawaii; Roach prefers Dana Point, California. Bodhi, who has been quietly listening off to the side while re-stringing an acoustic guitar (oh no, is he one of those bores who would play "Wonderwall" at a house party?) proclaims that Bells Beach, Australia, is the biggest surf he can think of. This causes some commotion within the gathering. Grommet insists, "No way Bells is bigger than Waimea, bro." "It will be next year," says Bodhi. Tyler, knowing what Bodhi is talking about, informs the rest of the group, "Bodhi believes the fifty-year storm is coming next year." Utah asks what is meant by this.

Minute 42

With the flames from the campfire flickering across the frame and lapping at his face, he explains.

> **Bodhi:** Everything moves in cycles. So, twice a century, the ocean lets us know just how small we really are. A winter storm comes out of Antarctica, tearing up the Pacific, and it sends a huge swell north 2,000 miles. And when it hits Bells Beach, it'll turn into the biggest surf this planet has ever seen. And I will be there.

The group becomes amped up at the prospect of surfing one of the most dangerous storms to impact a region in half a decade. Bodhi continues, noting that "If you want the ultimate, you gotta be willing to pay the ultimate price. It's not tragic to die doing what you love." The others then comment that this is the only way to go, with Grommet suggesting he will not live past thirty years of age. Bodhi looks pleased with himself that his philosophies have landed on enthusiastic ears. His minions are sold on his death-trip idealism. Tyler only sees tragedy and inflated male egos. "There's too much testosterone here," she comments as she gets up and leaves the firepit. She trails a hand across Utah's shoulder as an instruction for him to come and find her.

We arc getting our first insight into the darker elements of Bodhi's spirituality. The "find yourself and lose yourself" philosophy that he bestowed on Utah mutates into a narcissistic persona in which "losing yourself" might mean losing your life to access some kind of nirvana and taking those around you to a watery grave as well. Tyler, well-versed in the macho boasts, schemes, and ego trips, understands this.

Yet, Bodhi's supposed deep thinking, which is impressive to his comrades, is a borrowed philosophy. His quips about "dying for what you love" and "paying the ultimate price" are actually attributed to Mark Foo, a Singapore-born, Hawaii-raised surfer who pioneered big-wave riding in the 1980s and tragically died (though he would not have thought so) on December 23, 1994, while doing what he loved—surfing the large breaks at Mavericks, California.[49] Bodhi's co-opting of Foo's philosophy shows him to be a man with no thoughts or ideas of his own. He is just that bit smarter, more persuasive, and more charismatic than those around him, able to pull in a group of acolytes to his cause.

According to surf journalist Chas Smith, on an average day Bells Beach has "one of the best waves in the whole wide world."[50] Average conditions call for "6ft to 8ft swells. It is not uncommon to see 15ft pulses," with a wave that "isn't known for its barrel" but its "wide, steep and strong"[51] face. The fifty-year storm strengthens these already dangerous conditions, meaning only the most skilled (and the most impulsive) surfer can tackle these kinds of waves.

As previously discussed, it is hard to watch *Point Break* today without also consciously or unconsciously incorporating into the narrative the climate crisis we face today. This crisis, as discussed earlier, and by no means purposely included at the time of the film's release, nonetheless looms large. Storms and other extreme weather events such as floods and fires that were once considered "once in a lifetime," "once-in-a-generation," or "one-in-100-years" have increased in frequency, now occurring once every decade, if not every couple of years. Watching the film today, with knowledge of climate-related catastrophic events, Bodhi's fifty-year storm at Bells Beach, which would have been considered "once in a lifetime" a few decades ago, could now be an almost biannual event.[52]

Minute 43

After a few minutes of hearing about Bodhi and his crew's surf stories and the prominence of near-death experiences they have had in the past or hope to have soon, I suspect that Bodhi's comment about Warchild and his gang of thugs only living to "get radical" might have been better applied to him and his own company. The crew seems intent on increasing the danger levels for themselves and getting more "radical" with their pursuits than what we have seen of Warchild's gang.

Utah decides to leave the firepit and follows Tyler. He finds her browsing Bodhi's candle-lit den, where she is studying photographs and mementos from his various trips and adrenaline-fueled exploits around the world. When Utah approaches, she states, "I hope you're not buying into this banzai bullshit like the rest of Bodhi's Moonies." Utah feigns ignorance, but Tyler continues: "You've got that kamikaze look, Johnny. I've seen it. Bodhi can smell it a mile away. He'll take you to the edge." Tyler's use of the term "Moonies" might imply that Roach, Grommet, and Nathaniel are more akin to cult members than actual friends. The term has insinuations to The Unification Church, a religious movement founded in 1954 by Sun Myung Moon in Seoul, South Korea. Followers of the church are referred to as "Moonies," and the church has often been insinuated to be a cult.[53] Are we being led to believe that Bodhi's hold over his gang is less as a friend and comrade and more as a cult-like leader?

Suddenly, and almost magically, Bodhi menacingly appears in the room. "Johnny has his own demons. Don't you, Johnny?" he says.

Minute 44

There is no time for Utah to answer as Bodhi is joined by the rest of the gang, who all seem excited. Bodhi hands Utah a black shiny surfboard that hangs up on his wall and suggests a "little stealth mission" to finish off the evening's festivities. As Utah holds the surfboard against the side of his body, his face is reflected on the polished black surface. We see two Utahs staring back at us, and in reality, we are also witnessing two Utahs operating simultaneously on screen. The Utah who is the FBI agent working undercover to infiltrate the surf community and the Utah who is actively embracing this new carefree existence and its accompanying philosophical elements. The way this shot is lit also places half of Utah's face in shadow and the other in light. Is this a way to stress the bubbling conflict within him?

We cut to a dark wall of waves that swells and crashes on the shore. Bodhi and his gang, along with Utah and Tyler, pull up to the beach in their beat-up trucks. They approach the maw of the surf. Utah comments to Tyler that he "can barely do this in broad daylight," to which she jokingly replies, "At least nobody's gonna see how bad you are."

It is an interesting contrast between the nurturing dispositions of Tyler and Bodhi's tutelage of Utah. When Tyler teaches him to surf, it is mechanical and instructional. She gets him to learn balance and posture before even getting wet. Bodhi, on the other hand, throws Utah into one of the most dangerous situations any surfer, even an experienced one, could face. This demonstrates that Bodhi wants Utah to tap into a survivalist instinct that will propel his adrenaline to higher levels. He wants Utah to skip past all the beginner stages of learning to surf and become addicted to the dopamine rush of hitting the waves.

Back on the beach, we see a hand holding a knife stab at a carton of fire fuel and pour the liquid contents over a handful of stacked blocks of wood.

The group of surfers paddle out into the tide. This surfing allows Utah an opportunity to surf by osmosis. This, according to Grant W. Kuhns, is essential to the act of surfing. He explains that "a good portion of learning to surf seems to be accomplished by emulating others."[54] Although how much can be emulated in this darkness is up to the imagination. This is not the point. Bodhi does not want Utah to "see" the surf or the other surfers; he wants him to "feel" it.

We return to the firestarter on the beach who ignites the wood gathered in a makeshift firepit. This character, referred to as Rosie (Lee Tergesen), hangs on the periphery of the crew. We caught a brief glimpse of him during the beach football game. Rosie is not a surfer, although he shares a similar look to the rest of the group. He appears a little older, tougher, and meaner. He dresses like a member of a biker gang or a singer in a death metal band. The knife he carries is of great concern, and it might not be the last we see of it. While the boys, along with Tyler, hit the surf, Rosie sits by his fire, dangling his leg in the flames and laughing maniacally while spitting beer toward the burning wood to ignite a flare of bright orange. It is telling that the rest of the crew live for the water and the spiritual connections to the ocean and nature, while Rosie seems more in awe of flames and causing himself mild pain.

Minute 45

It is almost pitch black on the waves. Only the shimmering moonlight offers illumination to the surfers and their activities. The swells are massive; they vibrate thunderously on the soundtrack. Utah paddles up to Bodhi. "I gotta be fuckin' crazy," he says. Bodhi responds, "But are you crazy enough?" Tyler, back in Minute 24, seemed to suggest that Utah might be "crazier" than Bodhi. He may or may not be, but he must prove his fearlessness to Bodhi in order to be accepted into the community—and to discover who the Ex-Presidents really are.

The surfers take to the waves. In this darkness, their only reliance is on proprioception and the vestibular sense; all other senses are detuned or dampened. Bodhi instructs Utah, "Just feel what the wave is doing, then accept its energy. Get in sync, then charge with it. You don't need to see." Utah sarcastically replies that vision is overrated.

Utah's blind lessons on the dark waves recall Luke Skywalker (Mark Hamill) in *Star Wars: A New Hope* (1977), when he first grasps his lightsaber and Jedi Master Obi-Wan Kenobi (Alec Guinness) instructs him to "let go of your conscious self and act on instinct," as he trains to deflect laser bolts from a floating droid. With a blast-shield visor covering his eyes, Luke manages to deflect a few blasts and, like Utah, takes the "first step into a larger world." It may stretch the metaphor to suggest that Utah's surf training mirrors Luke's path to becoming a Jedi Knight and mastering the Force, yet both men must surrender to a process they do not fully understand. Each must allow his body to yield to a greater natural power (Utah to the waves, Luke to the Force) and trust in the guidance of a mentor.

In an article for *MEL* Magazine, writer Andrew Fiouzi recounts his own experiences with night surfing and how, after one particularly hazardous session a month or so after his thirtieth birthday, he decided to withdraw from the activity altogether. Fiouzi notes that "there's a subculture of masculinity—for better or worse—that doesn't operate under the premise that more muscle means more manly. Instead, peacocking comes in the form of engaging with fear."[55]

This is what Bodhi and his gang are doing during their night surf: an exercise in masculine showboating. Yet they seem so accustomed to it that genuine fear no longer plays a factor. At the same time, they are assessing Utah, measuring his fear, testing whether he can endure both the experience and the unspoken intimidation of the group. This is Utah's initiation ritual.

Minute 46

Bodhi spies an oncoming wave and calls out to Utah, "This one's got your number on it." He instructs him to paddle hard toward it. Utah puts aside his apprehension and pushes forward to meet the surge. Alongside Bodhi, he leaps onto his board and rides the swell with surprising skill, managing to stay upright and glide smoothly along its crest. Bodhi whoops in encouragement. "Is this not the best feeling on Earth?" he shouts over the thunderous crash of the waves. The musical score swells with a sense of pure elation.

Sean Redmond notes that these particular night surf sequences show "Utah's body is opened up and moves through liminal spaces. Blood rushes through his veins, muscle and bone are tested, his inner spirit comes into existential being, on the wild, free, and expansive surf."[56]

Utah has broken through a barrier, not just in the act of surfing but within himself, gaining insight into the function of his own body, how it moves with the waves, and the emotions that resonate.

In his book *Surfing and Sartre: An Aquatic Inquiry into a Life of Meaning*, philosopher and surfer Aaron James notes that "the surfer flows through different wave moments, moving from one moment to another and then to the next, which is quickly coming. And just as each span of a person's whizzing wind of experience is unique and non-repeatable, each wave is its own complex moment, calling for a fresh adaptation of flowing ability, bodily movements, and stylish self-presentation."[57]

This is the lesson that Bodhi is bestowing upon Utah tonight. Unlike Tyler, Bodhi has given Utah permission to feel the waves and feel something within himself grow. Surfing in the darkness allows him not to rely so heavily on his eyes, but to tap into the feeling of his own bodily movements as they flow with the varying wave formations.

Minute 47

In discussion with her then-husband, director James Cameron, and recorded for *American Film* by Tom Johnson, Bigelow considers this moment as Utah's evolution away from the so-called "black and white western philosophy" of his education and FBI training toward the more spiritual world of surfing and his immersion into "a lifestyle that is diametric to everything he has known." Within this embrace, Utah, according to Bigelow, "gains a soul."[58]

Back at the beach, Rosie is still drinking and dangling parts of his body over the fire pit. Bodhi and his gang emerge from the dark wall of the ocean. The gang leaves the fire for Utah and Tyler, and they go to get some food. Utah and Tyler remain in the waves.

Minute 48

We can visually witness the moment Utah attains his soul while drifting on the calm, dark ocean. Tyler, who approaches him on her own surfboard, chuckles and verbally acknowledges the change in him: "I'd say you looked almost happy." Utah responds, "I can't describe what I'm feeling." They look at each other while floating on the dark waters. Utah leans in toward Tyler. They share a long and passionate kiss. The scene switches to a view from underneath the two surfboards, with the gentle moonbeams penetrating the water. The perspective is similar to when Tyler swept in under the waves and rescued Utah from drowning. Here, though, the two are situated on surfboards, and there is no saving. They are both equal.

Perhaps it is the Gen-X proto-grunge aesthetics of the characters, the appearance of Anthony Kiedis of the Red Hot Chili Peppers, and James Le Gros's role in the seminal grunge film *Singles* (1992) that makes me think about what may be occurring a few miles down the coastline in San Diego, California, around the same time that *Point Break* was being filmed in Malibu. These waters that wash up on shore and the waves that Utah and Bodhi glide over are the same as those that a young, then-unknown rock vocalist and gas station attendant named Eddie Vedder also navigated as an enthusiastic surfer. As Utah sits on the waves and soaks up newfound inspiration, Vedder, living in San Diego at the time, received a cassette tape of raw instrumental music from a group of Seattle-based musicians looking to recruit a vocalist for their new band. The tape was passed to Vedder by his friend and former Red Hot Chili Peppers drummer Jack Irons, who thought the band might be a good fit. After absorbing the music during a quiet overnight shift at the gas station and having had no sleep, Vedder hit Tourmaline Surf Park for an early morning surf. Years later, he told *CBS* "I remember it being super foggy. One of those days when you think you won't go out. But I had the music in my head, the instrumental. I just kind of wrote it and I was still wet when I hit 'record.'"[59]

The lyrics to three of the songs that made up the cassette came to Vedder while out on the misty surf. These songs, titled "Alive," "Once," and "Footsteps," formed a mini-rock opera that Vedder referred to as the Momma-Son trilogy. Once the tape was sent back to Seattle, the recordings secured Vedder a place as lead vocalist and chief lyricist with the band that would become Pearl Jam within a matter of weeks, and subsequently, a role as a voice of a generation and an advocate for ocean sustainability and preservation. I find it fitting that a fictional portrayal of a person tapping into their inner self on screen through surfing can be connected and mirrored to a real-world moment that evokes the same thoughts and feelings of "finding a soul." Coincidentally, *Point Break* hit cinemas in July 1991. Pearl Jam's debut record *Ten* came out the following month. It might be a different break, but the same ocean washed over Vedder that washes over Utah here at this moment.

Minute 49

It is now morning. The camera pans over the surfboards discarded in the sand, along with a smoking firepit and some abandoned beer bottles. We find Utah and Tyler wrapped up in a blanket, asleep on the beach. Momentarily, we are unsure if only Tyler is asleep, as her jet-black hair blends with Utah's own. A squawking seagull wakes him with a start. He rises from behind Tyler in a panic and tries to locate his watch. "Holy shit!" he exclaims. He is late for the raid at the surf punk's residence. His expletive jolts Tyler awake, and he struggles to get his jeans on. But this is not the Blue Flamer from earlier in the film. The old Utah would have set his alarm clock, had a restful sleep, eaten a healthy breakfast, showered, and been ready and alert. The new Utah is less concerned about this. He laughs at his own relaxed attitude as he pulls on his jeans and leans over to kiss and caress Tyler as she lies in the sand. It is obvious that his feelings for her are real.

Minute 50

The canoodling continues. Utah gets up to leave but falls back down with a laugh to kiss Tyler one last time. He is late; he has

FBI agents waiting for his arrival, yet he seems not to care. He has engaged with a different perspective of the world, where time and place are irrelevant.

This idyllic beach scene offers another example of a rare but necessary "rest note" within the film, an opportunity to disengage from the relentless narrative flow. The peace is abruptly interrupted by Utah's beat-up car screeching along a hot, dirty-looking suburban backstreet. It is so hot, in fact, that the air shimmers through a thick, choking heat haze. It is only a few hours after sunrise, and already the humidity has built up. Utah pulls up and exits the car with a gun in his hand. He grabs a walkie-talkie from Pappas's vehicle, which is parked just across the alleyway. He takes a back route behind the houses and joins Babbit and Alvarez, who are positioned with guns ready, awaiting further instructions. Utah is greeted by Babbit. "I can't believe you're late to your own raid. What a flake!" he says.

Minute 51

We now enter into a sequence that will occupy the film for the next ten minutes and mark a significant turning point for the remainder. Up to this moment, we have seen very few full-blown action scenes. The film, while maintaining its swift pace, has also flowed through a series of scenes that offer limited fragments of what might be considered action cinema. The bank robbery by the Ex-Presidents, all the way back in Minute 7, was exhilarating and shot and edited with a sense of kinetic energy and excitement, but it was also over quickly. The scenes of surfing dotted throughout the film have offered thrills but have mostly been photographed in glacial slow motion, emphasizing the tranquility felt by those participating in the activity. There has been one brutal fight, again, over within a minute or so and tinged with some humor. The next ten minutes will be a centerpiece of action cinema.

We are aware that we are in the midst of an action film, but it is only through the limited scenes of violence that we truly know it. The rest is felt through the rapid editing techniques, the soundtracks, and lusty performances. We feel the shift in this minute as the narrative takes a darker turn and begins its crawl toward an inevitable confrontation between Utah and the Ex-Presidents.

Pappas gets on the radio and asks if Utah has finally arrived. "Very good of you to show up, hotshot," Pappas says sarcastically as he wires up. Utah grabs the radio and asks what the game plan is.

Pappas: Okay, here's how it is. Babbit and Alvarez are gonna go in the back door. Cullen's (another FBI agent) gonna back me up. I want you at the side window by the hedge. Now you're strictly back up. I don't wanna burn your cover.

Utah affirms his position. His exuberance for the operation feels like overcompensation for his lateness. The roles have switched. He is now a surfer pretending to be an FBI agent.

Pappas gives the order over the radio to begin and starts walking along the street, shouting for a dog named "Scooby"; he is pretending to have lost.

Minute 52

We follow Utah as he ducks, dives, and weaves through the overgrown garden surrounding the surf punks' house. The camera follows and hovers as if it is another agent shadowing him. The last time the camera moved with this much jittery energy was during the brief bank robbery in Minute 7. Does this mirrored camera motion connect to the Ex-Presidents lounging unaware in the house?

Babbit and Alvarez move to the back door, their jackets prominently adorned with the FBI logo on the backs. Alvarez peers through a window and sees one of the punks, though not one we recognize from the beach fight or the surf sequence, gleefully pouring what appears to be a can of beer into a bowl of Cheerios. Both agents assume a position on each side of the back entrance.

Pappas marches up to the house, still calling for his lost dog. He knocks on the front door. Utah maintains his position in the hedges by the side of the house. He takes out a small retractable mirror from his pocket and extends it above the fence. He spots Tone, the useless-in-a-fight surf punk from Minute 34 and 35, lying in bed in a pair of Union Jack boxer shorts and listening to some hard rock music on his headphones while the figure of a woman showers in the bathroom. Utah jumps out of his skin (and on first viewing, so do we) and pulls his gun as a next-door neighbor starts up a noisy lawnmower. He takes a deep breath, calms himself, and sends the retractable mirror back above the fence once again.

Minute 53

Utah watches in his tiny mirror as Warchild and Bunker burst into Tone's room and shake him out of his music listening enjoyment. They tell him that there is someone at the door and to get the guns. Tone empties a small armory of weapons onto his bed.

Pappas keeps banging at the door, and eventually a woman, referred to as Fiberglass (Kimberly Martin), dressed only in her underwear, answers. Utah sees the gang tossing guns to each other and calls Cullen on the radio to pull Pappas out. "They're pulling out a fuckin' arsenal," he shouts over the broadcast. The powerfully loud lawnmower engine drowns out Utah's voice. The punks, locking and loading their weapons, are in a panic.

Minute 54

The momentum of this minute is pure chaos. We are thrown around from three distinct locations: Utah, panicking just outside the window; the surf punks throwing weapons toward each other in the bedroom; and Pappas arguing loudly about his little lost dog with Fiberglass at the front door. Each location is noisy with chatter or churning lawnmowers. A jittery camera remains in the bedroom with the punks, watching the interaction at the door. The soundtrack creates a slow build of rising and fading synth, with spasms of percussion. This tense music drops out completely as Pappas finally pulls out his FBI badge and forces himself into the house. A storm of gunfire rages. Close to an hour into the film, the realization kicks in that this is the first wave of extreme gunfire we have heard since those opening minutes when Utah shot at paper targets on a gun range.

Fiberglass is thrown down while standing in front of Pappas. Utah pops his head through the window and shouts, "FBI, drop it," but is shot at by Bunker. He whips his head out of sight just in time. The woman showering in Tone's bathroom, referred to as Freight Train (Julie Michaels), screams as bullets shatter her shower screen and spray her with glass. Utah leans back in and guns down Bunker. Warchild enters the fray and fires bullets toward Utah. He ducks past the still-frantically screaming Freight Train and takes up a position.

Babbit and Alvarez, hearing the commotion, break through the back door and enter the kitchen area. The surf punk who was chowing down on beer and Cheerios raises his hands as if to surrender, but also as if to plead with them to stop the operation. The agents jump on him anyway, force him to the ground, and handcuff him.

Minute 55

Pappas confronts Archbold, the surf punk formerly mistaken for Flea, as he tries to escape with a captive and injured Fiberglass. Pappas fires a bullet into Archbold's head.

Back in the bedroom, Utah and Warchild are still trading shots across the room. The still screaming and naked Freight Train attacks Utah and beats him. As Babbit and Alvarez charge into the house to help, the two agents bust a door wide open, trapping Tone behind it. The pressure of the door jamming against his body and the wall causes him to shoot a bullet into his own foot. He screams in pain, a cry that bleeds over the noise of the raid for the remainder of the minute. Freight Train then approaches Babbit and stabs him in the back. Pappas intervenes and knocks her out cold.

Minute 56

The movement of the scene is unbelievably fast, yet in no way disorienting. Warchild and Bunker's house is a mess of stifling air, splattering blood and glass, and ricocheting bullets, but there is also a coherent floor plan to the action, and we know where we are and what perspective we have at all times.

Discussing this sequence with Gavin Smith for *Film Comment*, Bigelow mapped out how she approaches these chaotic scenes without sacrificing spatial awareness.

> I think geography is so important in action sequences. I see a lot of films in which geography is sacrificed, it's just a lot of fast cutting, a lot of noise, a lot of impacts-and I have no idea where I am, or who's coming from the left or right. So I start with storyboards. I usually have a foam core model built and work the pieces; sometimes I'll do video animatics to see the angles and see how it works and then I keep compressing and compressing it in the boards, pulling

> shots out to see how tight I can make it yet be completely oriented.[60]

This is one of Bigelow's greatest strengths as a director of action sequences. She ensures the audience is placed at the center of the action, able to feel the scramble and noise of the scenes by placing the camera in line with the perspectives of those involved and securing "a tremendous amount of coverage"[61] of the events to ensure there is always an interesting perspective to cut to. The audience is not just a distant observer of the chaos; they feel like they are there, potentially in danger of physical harm.

The last thug standing is Warchild, who thinks he can make an escape through the bedroom window, but Utah spots him, lunges across the room, and they both crash through the glass onto the lawn, which, despite the gunshots and other commotions occurring, is still being tended to by the neighbor.

Utah and Warchild fight while the lawnmower engine and blades churn away. Warchild pulls out a knife. Utah drags Warchild to the ground and pushes the hand holding the knife into the rotating lawnmower blades. The knife is flicked away. This gives Warchild the idea to pulp Utah's face against the fast-twisting blade of the lawnmower. He gains the upper hand and slowly pushes Utah's body down.

This fight emerges as one of the most overtly homoerotic engagements within a film that already provides plenty of opportunity for implied homoeroticism. Warchild is positioned directly behind Utah, chest exposed, a glaze of sweat running across his body. At another point, Utah is placed directly on top of Warchild, and they clasp hands above their heads, their faces just inches apart. As Warchild attempts to chop Utah up with the lawnmower (a grisly act even for a sadistic surf punk), he positions himself on his knees behind him while Utah is bent over, his rear end pressed against Warchild's crotch. Add to this the orgasmic grunts and groans from both men, the hair pulling, the slick glaze of sweat on Warchild's exposed chest, and the expressions of pained anguish on both men's faces, and this so-called "fight" could be mistaken for a scene from a gay pornographic film.

Minute 57

The climax of the scene, in this case Utah's face colliding with the lawnmower rotor blades, is interrupted by Pappas firing his gun to knock out the engine. The chaotic soundscape that has been a feature of this entire sequence ends abruptly as Pappas arrests Warchild, while Utah stomps up and down the lawn, letting the adrenaline in his body dissipate. He looks almost disappointed at the outcome—or should that be unsatisfied by it? Is this the end of his undercover assignment? The arrest of Warchild is anticlimactic for Utah. He apprehended a man, but he has not seized the real object of his affection.

We cut back to the house, where Tone is being treated for a blown-off foot, and Bunker is being wrapped up in a body bag. Utah is in the bathroom, cleaning up from his confrontation with Warchild. He looks at himself in the cracked mirror, contemplating his actions. Is he cut out for such violence? Surfing has cleansed his soul, giving him a new perspective on life that taps into a clarity he has never experienced before. If the life of an FBI agent is to crush the human spirit of those he pursues and extinguish his own while performing his duties, is it worth it? Sean Redmond notes that this scene is revealing for several reasons. Utah is "queasy" at the thought that his gun has been used to kill someone. He is nauseous at the "sight of blood." This gives Utah a supposed feminine trait. Yet, Utah, unlike other action heroes, is a so-called "new man, flawed like every man, vulnerable to attack, reliant on others (male and female) to keep him from harm, and keenly aware of the meaning and sanctity of human life."[62] The casting of Reeves as the hero, and Swayze as the antagonist, subverts the archetype represented in action films of the previous decade. With his feminine traits and boyish moniker, Utah is, according to Katherine Barscay, "no action hero," and his "delicate features, actively code him as a character that evokes aspects of femininity."[63]

The films of the more atypical action stars Arnold Schwarzenegger, Sylvester Stallone, and Bruce Willis feature excessive violence, unsympathetic death scenes, noisy gunfire, and defusing one-liners. The mental toll of killing, maiming, and torturing those who stand in their way is never a feature of these films. Take, for example, director Mark L. Lester's *Commando* (1985), which stars Arnold Schwarzenegger at his absolute peak physical form. In this film, Schwarzenegger portrays former Special Forces Colonel John Matrix, who embarks on a mission to rescue his young daughter after she has been kidnapped by an old foe. Matrix takes on a group of henchmen and an entire legion of armed troops, killing, maiming, and dispatching them with gleeful one-liners and smirks. When he saves his daughter, he carries her through the carnage he has left behind without shielding her eyes or explaining his actions. He is desensitized to violence, and this desensitization can be passed along to his young daughter.

It is telling, though, that Schwarzenegger began to temper these violent characteristics as the so-called "new man" actors, represented by the likes of Reeves and Swayze, came to the fore in the 1990s, and the machismo of the Reagan/Bush era bled into the softer (at least on the surface) Clinton era. Schwarzenegger appeared as a cop turned kindergarten teacher in the action-comedy *Kindergarten Cop* (1990) and revisited his role as the unfeeling cyborg in director James Cameron's *Terminator 2: Judgment Day* (1991), but this time his character was that of a protector and compassionate father figure to the young John Connor, not his killer.

Utah realizes his actions may have consequences for himself and others. He understands that those left dead have loved ones and people who may have cared for them. That this is allowed to be acknowledged within the confines of an action film is subversive. Yet even the casting of Reeves as the action hero, and the handsome Swayze as the antagonist, is also a subversive act.

Through the busted mirror reflection, we see Pappas approach Utah from behind, aware of the conflict raging within him. His positioning just over Utah's left shoulder gives the impression of a good angel offering guidance. Interestingly, Utah's right shoulder is completely out of shot. Who lingers on the hidden opposing shoulder? Bodhi? Tyler? Or the surfer Utah?

"It's been paper targets up until today, huh?" Pappas asks. He is clearly upset that he downed Bunker and that others in the house have died or been injured. The interior of the house surrounding them has been blown to pieces by the skirmish. Destruction is everywhere. Pappas continues his reassuring talk, something he learned from his Vietnam commanders. "It's no different, Johnny. Just a little more to clean up," he states. Of course, it is vastly different. The physical "clean up" of the space might be taxing, but only for a few hours. The mental "clean up" in dealing with the trauma may take years or may never happen at all.

Minute 58

This calm moment of partner-to-partner bonding, another "rest note" within the film, is abruptly interrupted by one of the surf punks aggressively bursting into the bathroom. This is the same punk seen earlier eating his bowl of Cheerios with beer before the raid started. Will he be seeking vengeance for his fallen comrades? Perhaps not, as Harp also enters the room, looking about as happy as he always does. The punk angrily reveals to Utah and Pappas that he is in fact Agent Dietz, a deep undercover operative for the Drug Enforcement Administration (DEA). He explains that he has been using his connection to the surf punks for the past three months to track down the main supplier of the crystal meth they have been casually selling on the streets and beaches of Los Angeles. He is indignant that his operation has been blown. Dietz, like Utah, has been acting undercover, but he has had the opposite experience. "You think I like this hair? You think I like these clothes?" he aggressively asks the two FBI agents. Utah, on the other hand, enjoys his new hair, new clothes, and new attitude to life. With no spiritual connection to the surf or the Zen lifestyle, Dietz is burned out, paranoid, and on the brink of mental collapse.

Dietz gives Utah and Pappas a rundown of the surf punks' movements and whereabouts over the past three months. Things do not add up. The Ex-Presidents robbed Tarzana City National Bank in the San Fernando Valley on August 2, but Warchild and his gang were in Fort Lauderdale, Florida, that same day, picking up a batch of meth to bring back home. The surf punks are not the Ex-Presidents. Harp is extremely displeased, but rather than deliver a lecture, he leaves the room with Dietz.

Minute 59

We cut to Utah and Tyler lying in bed together. Tyler is fast asleep, lying on her front with her arm draped across Utah's chest. The blanket rides across their midriffs. Utah's arm is raised above and behind his head. They are entangled together. Utah is wide awake, staring at the ceiling in deep contemplation. He rhythmically strokes Tyler's arm in an act of comfort. The shock of seeing Utah bare-chested becomes apparent to the viewer. So far, we have not seen him stripped to the waist like this. During all the surfing scenes, he wore a wetsuit. Though muscular and toned, his skin is also soft, and his upper body, almost entirely hairless. That remark about "little rubber people who don't shave yet" from earlier comes to mind. The camera slowly descends from the ceiling toward his face. The doorbell rings, breaking him out of his pensive thoughts and waking Tyler from her slumber. Katherine Barscay notes that this image of Utah and Tyler in bed together is "staged almost like a painting, shocking the viewer when it is disrupted by the sound of the doorbell."[64] Bigelow once again offers a momentary rest note after an extremely chaotic sequence within the film has just transpired. Yet just as the pause in the action begins to feel sustained, she brings the audience back into the narrative with a jolt.

Minute 60

Utah checks the football helmet clock on his bedside table. It reads 4:56 a.m. The buzzing persists, growing more impatient. Utah gets out of bed and opens the door to find Bodhi and the gang standing there. Has news reached them about the raid at Warchild's house? Do they know it was led by Utah? If it has, Bodhi doesn't show it. Instead, he insists that Utah and Tyler join them for the "five-foot walls at Zeros." Zeros refers to a particularly potent surf spot at Nicholas Canyon Beach in Malibu. Tyler sleepily sighs, "He does this," as they grab their boards, wetsuits, and head out for an early morning surf.

We cut to wild waves, frothy and full of spray and mist. The weather is beginning to shift toward the cooler months of early fall. The surfing season is almost over. The pursuit of the Ex-Presidents will have to conclude as soon as they "travel on the money" and "disappear like ghosts." Bodhi and the gang are out on the surf, already enjoying the waves, while Utah and Tyler stroll along the beach. With his mind still on the botched raid from the previous day, Utah observes the four men on the water, moving with a synchronicity he has never noticed before.

Revelation

Minutes 61–119

Minute 61

We have arrived at approximately the halfway point of the film. Utah has finally registered what we the audience have always suspected or expected: that Bodhi and his gang of spiritual surf dudes are the Ex-Presidents he has been looking for. Grommet, after taking on a radical curve, suddenly drops his shorts to jovially reveal his buttocks to the rest of the gang. This image has been ingrained in Utah's mind since seeing LBJ's rear end on the surveillance screen during the first robbery he witnessed earlier in the film, though the words "Thank You" are missing this time. This is the moment in which the realization hits. The spiritual calm and tranquil enlightenment advocated by Bodhi and his crew have masked their crimes and fooled Utah. As he stares out into the ocean, Tyler asks if he is okay. "You look like you saw a ghost," she says. Ghosts. We cut back to a flash of footage from when Utah and Pappas were casing the drop car, with Pappas imploring Utah to forget about the Ex-Presidents: "They are ghosts," he states.

I click back to this earlier moment on the progress bar. I want to verify whether the delivery of Pappas's line is from the same shot. It is not; it is a different take. This is fine, because we are led to believe it is a flash of memory from inside Utah's mind, and memories tend to diverge from how events actually occurred. What is apparent is the difference between Utah's appearance at this moment of realization and the man he was in this earlier scene.

Not that I want to break any illusions of how this book was written, but it has been several weeks since I watched this early part of the film. The events that have occurred between then and now have slowly unfolded as if the film were being read like a thick novel rather than a brisk action film. Not only that but I have also watched other films, seen other television shows, read some books and articles, and experienced other life events in the meantime. For a start, I am writing this segment in mid-July and am a little more suntanned than I was when I began the project. In a normal viewing period, these changes within the film would be barely noticeable. The hidden reality effect of film means that subtle changes go unacknowledged, as they should be. In this book's methodology of stop-and-start viewing and almost frame-by-frame analysis, familiarity with the characters' faces and their life circumstances makes seeing an earlier incarnation of them shocking. It is akin to meeting up with an old friend you have not seen in several years and realizing how much they have aged in the interim, how much the hair has receded, the added wrinkles on the face, the sagging jowls. They likely think the same of you. Here, though, the reverse is true. The Utah in the first few minutes of the film looks older than the one seen here. He has aged in reverse. The hardness and intensity of early Utah have dissipated into a more relaxed and, dare I say, happier version of himself.

All the clues are placed together in Utah's mind. Bodhi and his gang are ghosts on the waves, figures who will soon disappear without a trace. Utah makes an excuse to Tyler and leaves.

Considering *Point Break* is so often referred to as a "surfer" film, this will be the last surfing we see until the very final moments, and it is certainly the last surf we will see in its idyllic setting. We are leaving behind the elements that provide *Point Break* with its iconography and cult status and instead entering the zone of a much darker second half.

Utah meets up with Pappas after night has fallen, following a full day of tailing Bodhi.

Minute 62

Pappas can hardly believe that the "Zen surf master" is Utah's current suspect, but Utah tells him that he followed Bodhi all around town. He explains, "Bodhi went to Tower Records, buys some CDs, has lunch at Patrick's Roadhouse. He goes into the Assured Trust Savings and Loan. He's inside 20 minutes. The other guy, Roach, waited in the truck. They were scoping it out, right?"

The reference to Patrick's Roadhouse is an amusing nod to Swayze's iconic role as James Dalton, the buff bouncer of the Double Deuce club in director Rowdy Herrington's *Road House*. As a brief aside, the 2006 sequel, *Road House 2*, directed by Scott Ziehl, featured Gary Busey's son, Jake Busey, as the character Bill "Wild Bill" Decarie. Hollywood is a small town, and these connections, however inconsequential, are often fun in a "Six Degrees of Kevin Bacon" style connective game.

Pappas states that Bodhi and Roach could be scoping the bank for a robbery, or they could be cashing a final check before leaving town. But Utah persists: "Then they go back to their beach house, and they box up all their shit. See, summer's over. They load it in Bodhi's truck, and they take it to a public storage unit." Pappas believes they have already split, but Utah insists they need some traveling money. "Assured Trust tomorrow, next day, outside, latest. I definitely got a feeling on this," Utah confidently states. To which Pappas responds, "Last time you had a feeling, I had to kill a guy." Pappas is less concerned with the trauma of putting a bullet through a surf punk's head and more concerned about how it looks on his report back to Harp. He does, however, still trust Utah's instincts and agrees to pursue the lead.

Minute 63

We cut to the next day, where Utah and Pappas are sitting inside their parked car outside the Assured Trust building. There are only two of them on this stakeout. After the debacle over the raid on the surf punks' house, Harp probably no longer trusts Utah's gut instincts and has sent them alone. Pappas seems more interested in reading and laughing at the Calvin and Hobbes comics in the *L.A. Life* newspaper than keeping an eye on the bank door. He suddenly realizes that he is hungry and directs Utah to go and buy him two meatball sandwiches from a sandwich shop around the corner. As Utah reluctantly exits the car, Pappas makes sure that he heard his order of two meatball sandwiches.

At the sandwich shop, Utah orders the two meatball subs and a tuna on wheat bread for himself, along with two lemonades.

Minute 64

As he purchases his order, a 1984 Lincoln suddenly pulls up to the bank entrance, and the Ex-Presidents scramble out and enter the bank. Utah misses the entire moment as he collects his food and change from the counter and walks back to Pappas, who is still engrossed in the funnies.

It is interesting that the Ex-Presidents arrive in a Lincoln. The Lincoln Motor Company was founded by Henry Leland and his son Wilfred in 1917 in Detroit. Henry Leland was such a supporter of former President Abraham Lincoln that he named the company after him and, later in 1922, erected a statue of Lincoln outside the company headquarters.[1] The Ex-Presidents literally pull up in a car christened after an ex-president.

Utah arrives with the food order and gives Pappas a brief startle. Utah asks if he saw the red Lincoln pull up and the driver get out. "What Lincoln?" asks Pappas. They both look toward the parked Lincoln and see not Honest Abe, but the deformed rubber masks of LBJ, Nixon, Reagan, and Carter emerging from the bank doors with a bag of cash. Utah loudly instructs, "FBI. Freeze!" as he pulls his gun while running toward the gang. Nixon takes aim at Utah, but Reagan smacks the gun away.

Minute 65

As the Ex-Presidents pull off in the Lincoln, Utah opens fire, taking out the back window. Pappas pulls up in the car, and Utah jumps in. A frantic and chaotic car pursuit begins through the streets of Culver City. The Ex-Presidents, Reagan in the driving seat and masks still firmly affixed to their heads, drive as fast as the Lincoln will allow them. Nixon, still in his gruff "Nixonesque" speech, proclaims, "I think we're losing 'em." Utah and Pappas exchange a series of frustrated verbal jabs as the Ex-Presidents swerve and sway further down the busy road. We see the pursuit from many perspectives: inside both vehicles, from the street, and even from other random cars caught up in the chase. This further adds to the chaotic nature of the scene, much like the tumultuous sequence when the FBI invades the surf punks' house. Like in that sequence, we are never left disoriented by the jerky camera movements and rapid-fire edits.

Minute 66

Utah and Pappas continue the car chase. They weave along the road, trying to maintain a constant gain on the Lincoln. As they go through an underpass, Nixon believes the two agents have been left behind, only to see them emerge from the side. Both cars careen into one another. Utah and Pappas crash into a parking booth. The Ex-Presidents roll over some traffic spikes but continue with deflated tires. Utah exits the car and leaves Pappas to try to get the smoking vehicle moving. He proceeds on foot. Inside the Lincoln, Reagan declares to the others that it is time for an "emergency sanitation." By this, he means to cleanse the Lincoln of any fingerprints or other traces.

Minute 67

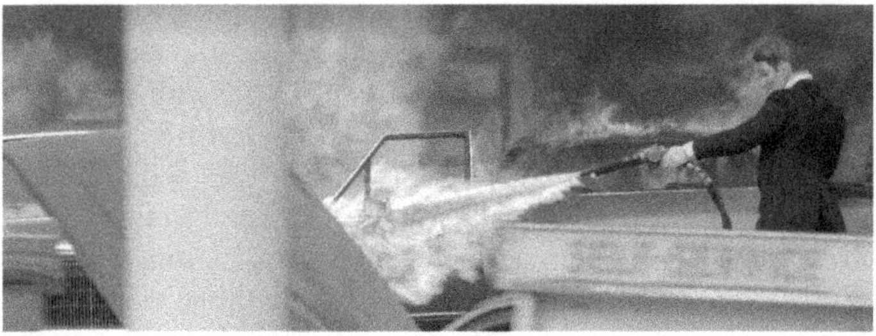

The Ex-Presidents pull into a gas station. Nixon, Carter, and LBJ scramble from the Lincoln and commandeer a Chevy from another customer. Reagan douses the Lincoln in gasoline and lights the nozzle. The image of Reagan flaming the Lincoln is a powerful one. The permanent and gruesome fixed grin of the mask ensures the image remains fixed in the mind of the audience. As the fire rises, it engulfs the floor, and thick black smoke emerges from the flames. As the other three members of the gang wait in the Chevy, the fire flickers across their image. Reagan is not just torching the Lincoln but the other presidents as well.

In a speech that the real Ronald Reagan gave on October 27, 1964, in support of the then-Republican presidential nominee Barry Goldwater, he stated, "You and I have a rendezvous with destiny."[2] That "destiny" would not be a Goldwater presidency. He was rejected by the American people the following month in favor of Lyndon B. Johnson. But it would eventually come to fruition for Reagan. He became governor of California in 1966 and began creating a path toward the presidency. It is also the case that Utah has a "rendezvous with destiny." It begins at this very moment.

As Reagan finishes the sanitation of the car and runs to join the others in the Chevy, Utah emerges from the flames, leaps over the burning vehicle, and brings Reagan down to the ground. They both roll through the flames. Pappas emerges and shoots out the back window of the Chevy. The others drive off in a panic, leaving Reagan behind.

Minute 68

With his tuxedo in flames, Reagan pushes Utah's body under a car hood and runs. We now embark on a foot pursuit that will last for the next several minutes and will see Utah and Reagan hotfoot it over and through the urban sprawl. The chaotic scene was shot using an innovative camera setup referred to as a "PogoCam," which consisted "of a very compact 35mm camera on a small rig, which is said to have been equipped with two gyro stabilizers at the bottom."[3] This allowed the film's camera operator, James Muro, to keep pace with the fleeing Reagan and the pursuing Utah, allowing the audience to enter the chase as a participant.

Luke Collins observes that this high-octane sequence offers a brief pause in the narrative, allowing the audience to experience the thrill ride of the action.

> The cinematography and editing stimulate adrenaline and while the catalyst for the release of this hormone is vicarious, the audience's experience of it in the body is primary. It is offered up again and again by the weightless fluidity of the camera movement and precise quick cuts. During the intensity of these sequences the narrative is suspended while

> both characters and audience are subsumed by the *affect* of the experience.[4]

The narrative is then "poised to unfold once the foot chase has been completed."[5] These kinetic scenes, more of which we will witness in the coming minutes, offer the opposite sensation of Bigelow's rest note but function on a similar level. They allow the audience respite from the narrative flow and provide sheer enjoyment and immersion instead.

Mark Isham's score kicks in as the chase gets under way. The music offers the first real sense of urgency we have heard, a "highly intense, percussive, and at times quite funky" composition that "allows groovy bass guitar rhythms to shine through."[6] The groove of the music propels Utah and Reagan through the streets.

Minute 69

We are a participant in the chase. We follow behind Reagan as he squeezes through tight alleyways, hops over fences, and runs through residents' houses and gardens, including splashing through a kiddie pool. We then join Utah through the same landscapes. Bigelow noted to Gavin Smith that the "chase as scripted was this incredible, relentless piece . . . That was my first glimmer of an unbroken sequence: even though there are cuts, it was almost constructed as if there were none."[7] There are plenty of editorial cuts, but they become barely noticeable for the viewer as the full immersion into the sequence becomes apparent, and we feel that we are running alongside the two men at a breathless pace. The chase connects to the environment around them, allowing for even more immersion into the scene. Both men interact with pedestrians and homeowners who get caught in the way. At one point, a pet dog is thrown by Reagan toward Utah as a distraction. The mutt is kicked away by Utah (thankfully, the kick is to a decoy stuffed animal, though a live dog was thrown). The mad barking continues to be heard in the distance as the chase continues.

Minute 70

The two men careen down a long slope and fall off a large wall into the dry Ballona Creek. The fall by both men is presented in slow motion. Reagan takes the landing well, picks himself up, and continues to run. Utah lands awkwardly on his knee and collapses in pain. He tries to get up and continue the pursuit but collapses once again. He pulls out his pistol, giving him at least the opportunity to incapacitate Reagan as he flees. Utah locks him in his aim. Realizing Utah cannot continue the chase, Reagan hangs on a high wire fence and looks back toward the injured agent. The two men eye each other for a moment. The camera draws closer to each face. Is this a show of desire? David Greven in his book *Manhood in Hollywood from Bush to Bush* thinks so, commenting that "the way Bigelow shoots the scene and uses parallel editing makes Utah's desire to possess Bodhi by looking at him palpable. Bodhi's gaze triumphantly refuses Utah's possessive one, even as Bodhi's eyes, the only visible aspects of him beneath the Reagan mask, hypnotically compel Utah to submit to him."[8]

Sean Redmond appears to agree with Greven that this moment is a realization for both men, stating that the stare-down is an act of "outing one another. Utah cannot shoot Bodhi and Bodhi knows this: they are in love with each other, and all that was once encoded male melts into air."[9]

Though we fully anticipate it, at this moment Utah (and the audience) is not even certain that Bodhi is the one behind the Reagan mask. After all, there has been no great reveal. Utah, convinced that the surf buddies he has been hanging with are the Ex-Presidents, could be chasing down Roach or Grommet for all he (or we) knows. We suspect or expect it to be Bodhi, based on casting alone. Yet Utah seems to know that it is Bodhi. The way in which the two men, according to Sam Raimer, "lock eyes on each other, their gaze snakes closer and closer with each cut."[10] indicates Utah knows Bodhi by his eyes and his longing gaze. For why would he have pursued him to such great lengths if he were not completely convinced? As we pull closer to Reagan's mask and it fills the frame, Bodhi's soulful eyes stare back from within the eyeholes. But with a separation of a few hundred yards, it would be impossible for Utah to discern those features.

Minute 71

Utah shoots his load, the bullets of his weapon, into the air in frustration, or, as Raimer suggests, a desperate act designed to "release himself" of his confused "homoerotic desires."[11] As we witnessed from the film's opening sequence, Utah's "100 percent" aim and execution of a loaded weapon could have taken Reagan out. It is a given that he allows him to jump the fence and escape. His struggle between his allegiance to the FBI and his embrace of the surfer lifestyle is tearing him up inside. Yet the desire to possess Bodhi is also confusing him. We see Reagan sprint away on foot. I managed to count fourteen bullets fired from Utah's gun. It is the perfect exhale of this relentless scene.

We return to the FBI offices, where another agent is running the plate number from the Chevy the Ex-Presidents stole and got away in. Utah sits beside him, nursing his bandaged knee. He is covered in cuts, bruises, and sweat, and totally removed from what is occurring around him. Pappas bursts into the room and asks Utah for a talk outside. He is clearly frustrated that Reagan and the rest of the Ex-Presidents got away. "I want you to know something," he states. "When you shoot, you don't miss." Utah insists that he shot but just missed. But Pappas is concerned; he knows something is wrong and calls Utah on it. "I believe you're either scared or you're getting too goddam close to this surfing guru buddy of yours," he says. Of course, it is the latter.

Minute 72

Pappas then leans in close. "I don't believe you're scared." Pappas tells Utah to go home and get some rest. He goes home, but Tyler joins him and helps him clean up his cuts. Utah again tells a lie about the circumstances of his injuries, claiming it was a "basic hit-and-run." We see Tyler tending to Utah's cuts and bruises from a close-up of Utah's face. Tyler's hand comes in and out of shot with pieces of bloody cloth to dampen the injuries. The camera then moves to the side to catch a view of Tyler in a mirror and a behind-the-head view of Utah reflected in it. Tyler seems to realize that something is not right about the story or Utah's current disposition. He does look tense and more like the man we met at the beginning of the film, with the stiff posture and uptight mannerisms. But there is now more to it. Utah has lied to his FBI partner, he has lied to Tyler, and maybe he is lying to himself. How much longer can Utah continue this charade?

Minute 73

We hear the murmurs of a confession almost drop from Utah's lips. He wants to tell Tyler the truth—that he is an undercover FBI agent. He almost does it. But Tyler takes the awkward attempt at a confession for a strained effort at a declaration of love toward her. She giggles, "Men are so bad at this." She places her fingers across his lips and tells him to try "some other time." She leans in for a kiss, and again the camera moves to the mirror reflection angle. Utah from behind looks much like Tyler from behind. The two merge. He looks like he is kissing a reflected vision of himself.

We cut to a tense-looking Bodhi staring directly into a roaring firepit on a darkened beach. The gang is arguing about what should happen next. Not only is Bodhi joined by Roach, Grommet, and Nathaniel, but Rosie also sits with them. Was he once "Ford" in the Ex-Presidents gambit? Or just a hired goon? Whatever his role, he is the more vicious of the bunch. He gleefully suggests he can "deal with that fuckin' cop," but Bodhi backs him off the idea. As things stand, there is still no definitive proof that Bodhi and his gang are the Ex-Presidents. No appearances were made during the chase scene. The masks stayed firmly on their heads throughout the encounter. The Lincoln was torched of fingerprints and other identifiable traces. In theory, there is nothing connecting Bodhi and the gang to the robberies except Utah's hunch. They, however, know for sure who Utah is. There is a great game to be played here.

Minute 74

Bodhi reminds the group that the bank robberies were never just about obtaining money but about going "against the system that kills the human spirit." Bodhi paints the Ex-Presidents as a modern-day Robin Hood outfit—taking from the rich to give to the poor. Except the Ex-Presidents are not as noble. They certainly take from the rich, but they give it to themselves, feeding their "endless summer" and ensuring their needs and desires are met and taken care of. Bodhi continues, much to the awe of his gang, "To those dead souls inching along the freeways in their metal coffins, we show them that the human spirit is still alive."

Though throughout history there have been examples of criminals and criminal gangs who have connected positively with the public and been celebrated for their notoriety—the Kray twins, D. B. Cooper, and Frank Abagnale, for example, I am not convinced that the Ex-Presidents are such an example.

Their crimes directly affect public safety. The mutated presidential masks create a barrier. The crimes are not acts of civil disobedience.

Grommet retaliates, admitting that he is scared and suggesting that they should skip town as soon as possible. Rosie, seemingly on board with Bodhi's framing, says that if they "run, you die." Bodhi asks the gang if they trust him.

Minute 75

"I know exactly what to do with him," Bodhi states. Yet his twitchy side-to-side eye movements suggest he is unsure of himself. We linger on Bodhi's flame-lit face for an uncomfortably long seven seconds. His eyes are wide, his brain working hard to put all the pieces together. Will he attempt to kill Utah or co-opt him into the gang?

We cut to a topless and sleeping Utah. A foreboding series of notes plays as the shadow of a drawn pistol crawls along the wall. The image, married to Isham's intense orchestral score, conjures up countless scenes from early film noir. The gun is pointed toward the still-sleeping Utah. Is this what Bodhi had in mind? Cold-blooded murder of an FBI agent? It seems like a big step up from bank robbery. The gun fires as the score peaks, and the bullet lands with a bang into the pillow next to where Utah's head lies. He wakes with a start. Tyler is revealed to be the one holding the gun. Surely this is attempted murder. She screams that Utah lied to her about his occupation. She throws his FBI badge onto the bed, which is covered in feathers from the blown-out pillow. She continues to point the gun in his direction and demands to know if he lied about his dead parents as well. With a gun on him, he has no choice but to admit that they are still alive and living in Ohio. He tells Tyler everything about the undercover operation, about how he needed her to get embedded within the surf community. She cuts him off with a hollered "Fuck you!" and then sincerely asks, "Don't you have a soul?" Utah has no answer for her. He is no longer sure if he does own a soul. She drops the gun on the floor.

Minute 76

Tyler runs out of the house. Utah attempts to run after her, but his injured knee buckles under him again, and he drops to the floor in pain.

We cut to a moment a little while later that shows Utah on the phone, leaving Tyler a voice message. He confesses all to her. He tells her why he could not reveal his identity. He then gets extremely frustrated with his own inadequacy: "Fuck! Why can't I ever say what I really mean?" Maybe because this confession is to the wrong person. Tyler is important to him, but really Bodhi is the one he wants to explain everything to. He calls again. Instead of watching this confession spill from Utah's lips, we only hear the monologue while we watch him lying on the bed asleep from above, shirtless, with the phone propped up on his stomach, awaiting Tyler's return call. It is a role reversal of the cliché female awaiting the male to call. But is he even really waiting for Tyler?

The doorbell buzzes. He believes Tyler has returned. When he opens the door, he is shocked to see Bodhi and the gang. They all look a little uncomfortable, but the masquerade of innocence must still be played out. Bodhi offers Utah a friendly "Howdy, bro." Utah asks what's going on. Bodhi, seeing the cuts on Utah's face, asks if he cut himself shaving. Utah states that he is not up to surf at this hour.

Minute 77

But surfing is far from Bodhi's mind. He has something more substantial planned. He charges around Utah's house in a rush and grabs clothing and boots for him to put on. Utah attempts to reach for the gun that Tyler discarded on the floor. He fails to obtain it before Bodhi rushes him out the door and into the waiting truck.

We cut to a small twin-engine plane sitting on a runway as the sun begins to rise. The propellers whirl with a loud roar. A pan shot across the landscape reveals Bodhi's truck driving up toward the plane. The gang unloads their equipment. Bodhi asks Utah if he has ever jumped from a plane before.

Minute 78

Utah confesses that he never has. Bodhi states that the act is "100 percent pure adrenaline. Other guys snort for it, jab a vein for it. All you gotta do is jump." Utah states that his busted knee will prevent him from jumping, but Bodhi, nonchalantly noticing the knee, reassures him that they will be landing on water. "Well fine then," he sarcastically replies, "I feel so much better." The false pretense is still being adhered to between the two men. They both act as if one of them were not in the eye of a gun barrel just yesterday.

Bodhi proclaims to the group, "Let's fly," and we switch to a shot of the plane taking off into the red, smoky-looking sky. The gang does one final safety check as they prepare to skydive. Bodhi tells Utah the dive is a ritual to end the summer season.

Utah suspiciously asks who packed his parachute. Bodhi says it was him and, with a wink to the others, asks, "Why? You don't trust me?" To which Utah responds, "You gotta earn trust." The gang goes back and forth, teasingly switching Utah's parachute a few times before he ends up with the exact same one in his hand. Utah asks the group if they "are gonna jump or jerk off?" The juvenile part of my brain immediately recalls a scene from episode 2 of season 4 of Seth Green and Matthew Senreich's Adult Swim animated series *Robot Chicken*, in which Utah, in tawdry stop-motion animated form, asks the same question to the gang. However, in this parody snippet, Bodhi and his associates are stopped in their tracks as the idea of "jerking off," instead of jumping lingers, and the plane side door abruptly shuts closed. The genius of the 16-second clip is the stop-motion Bodhi's unchanging and unblinking facial expression, and the sudden head tilts of the other stop-motion figures in the background. The closing of the plane door is a magnificent full stop to the clip. The short clip captures, in hilarious form, the homosocial and homoerotic undertones of the film itself, along with the underlying sexual tension between Utah and Bodhi. It begs the question: if the two men had been open about each other's feelings earlier in the film, the violence might have been reduced. Utah and Bodhi could have ridden off into the sunset together.

Minute 79

This is why I admire *Point Break* so much. It delves into a world and a series of activities I can never be a part of. As I divulged all the way back in Minute 1, I cannot surf, and no amount of intrigue in the sport or love of the water will ever get me up comfortably on a surfboard. The lifestyle, the freedom, the sun-kissed beaches, and the apparent lack of responsibilities all appeal to me—especially when the doldrums of capitalism hover like an ever-present dark cloud over most of my days. When I stated that I would jump through the screen to touch the sand and swim in the ocean, I was not lying. Even if just for a short reprieve.

Here, in this minute, we witness another activity that seems so far from my own comfort zone: skydiving. Flying has never been a form of travel I have appreciated. It remains a fear I have never truly conquered, though one I will tolerate in a state of absolute anxiety for the duration of the flight. When the wheels of the plane safely touch the ground, I am offered a wave of relief and elation akin to what the adrenaline junkies in *Point Break* feel numerous times throughout the day. Being inside a plane is bad enough, but jumping or falling out of one seems terrifying.

This is acknowledged by Roach, who states, "Johnny, you're about to jump out of a perfectly good airplane. How you feel about that?" There is no opportunity to answer. All five men leave the plane from the side door and tumble into the open air.

Minute 80

As the five men fall to the ground, the combination of visuals and the tranquil, euphoric score is astounding. The sheer blue sky is the brightest we have seen throughout the film. The landscape stretches out to the limitless horizon. The early morning sun shining on the lakes and ravines below makes them look crystal clear. Matched with the exuberant expressions of exhilaration on the faces of Bodhi, Utah, and the rest of the gang, the scene is one of the most tranquil we have witnessed within the film—possibly within any film, in fact. The earlier surf scenes offered moments of serenity, but the visible ocean often rendered these scenes a chaotic dance upon the waves. There was the knowledge that the riders had to navigate the swells with intention in order to remain afloat. Here, the air currents are invisible to us. The divers must give themselves over to the fall. They float, spin, and roll through the air and settle upon the landscape that endures behind them. It is magical. The Earth at this moment is truly breathtaking. The largeness of the planet and the smallness of the skydivers are astronomical.

Again, as before with the chase scene, the narrative pauses, allowing us to participate in the experiences. Luke Collins notes that "the velocity of the moment takes over and the audience is left to enjoy the pleasures of these extreme spectacles: spectacles that are carefully crafted to stimulate the viewer."[12]

The pleasure is amplified by knowing that Swayze himself participated in the jumps, and one can visually discern his features as he loops the loop in midair.

Minute 81

In an interview with American film critic Bobbie Wygant, Bigelow noted that she wanted the skydiving scenes to be an immersive experience for the audience. "My intent was to put the audience in as close to an experiential situation as possible. In other words, I wanted it all to be shot with as much movement as possible so that you're actually feeling the velocity that those people are feeling."[13]

For a full ten seconds, we pull onto a shot of Nathaniel relaxing on the air currents as if he were lounging in a La-Z-Boy chair. We return to a close-up of Utah, who is experiencing a more frenzied descent than Bodhi and the crew but still appears to be enjoying the ride. A wide shot from underneath shows the five men as specks against the bright blue sky. Bodhi begins to bring the boys together to form a circle formation, leaving a gap for Utah to glide himself into position.

Minute 82

Bodhi instructs Utah to "Fly like an eagle, baby." He joins the circle formation. It is the perfect image of male unity. We see the formation from below against the bright sky and from above as the Earth lingers ever closer. As they fall, Roach shouts, "How'd you like it, Johnny?" "Amazing," he cries in response, "Fucking amazing."

David Greven believes that this moment in the film marks a representation of "male sexual abandon." He continues to elaborate: "In the air, the men's bodies ecstatically whoosh and careen, and Utah momentarily loses all sense of prohibition and retribution, giving in completely to the exhilarating liberation of airborne homosocial bonding."[14] Indeed, Utah seems to forget that just a few hours earlier, he was chasing who he believed to be Bodhi through the suburban streets of Culver City with a gun drawn. He neglects to acknowledge that the men he holds onto as they form their bonding circle are armed thieves he has been actively pursuing for weeks. All of this seems to have escaped him as his thrill-seeking side takes over.

After a few moments, Bodhi orders the crew to break formation and spread out. He reaches his hand out to Utah, and the two clasp tightly as they continue to descend toward the lakes.

Minute 83

As a safe distance is reached, Grommet, Nathaniel, and Roach all pull their parachute cords and are briskly sent back up and out of frame. Bodhi and Utah continue to drop, their grip on each other's hands still intact. From a distanced, ground-based camera angle, we see the two men descend like smudged flies on a giant blue canvas. Bodhi clocks that the ground is 1,000 feet away and instructs Utah to pull his parachute cord. Utah insists that Bodhi should pull his first. The two continue to fall toward the lake below. Eventually, Bodhi reaches over to Utah's pack and pulls the cord for him, sending Utah, much to his annoyance, shooting upward into the sky while Bodhi maintains his masculine pride at being the last to pull his chute. Bodhi's parachute opens mere feet from the water. He drops in with a graceful splash, and his parachute flows over the top of the water. He emerges from the lake in slow motion, shakes his hair dry like a wet dog, and removes his goggles.

We have just witnessed an exhilarating and immersive sequence of film.

Minute 84

We see Utah hovering over the lake. He drops in with an awkward splash. He emerges from the water in the same fashion as Bodhi and notes to himself, "I gotta be losing it." The other three members of the crew gracefully drop into the lake. These past five minutes have felt truly exhilarating within a film that offers plenty of exhilaration and breathtaking moments.

As the five men walk across a dusty flat field carrying their parachutes, Bodhi states that skydiving is the "closest you'll ever get to God." They continue to exchange pleasant descriptions of the activity as they reach the plane taxied on the runway. They drop their packs on the tarmac. As previously mentioned, the descriptor Bodhi used for Warchild and his gang of surf punks about only living to "get radical" should also apply to Bodhi and his crew. They engage in far more radical activity than what we saw from Warchild and his comrades.

Minute 85

Bodhi casually pulls Utah aside from the rest of the group, claiming that there is "something you need to see." They walk toward a parked van. Bodhi tells Utah to hop inside and pulls out a portable viewing device, switching it on. When Utah asks what this is, Bodhi replies that it is "an insurance policy. It is going to sting a bit." He instructs Utah to press play on the device. On the monitor, we see an image of Tyler tied and gagged to a chair. She is being filmed by someone using a camcorder. She screams at the camera as it moves around her restrained body. The camera then pulls back to a wider shot, and in a reflection in the mirror, we see both her and Bodhi's reckless associate, Rosie, holding a knife to her throat. Her eyes never look away from the camera's gaze. It is a shocking image to behold, made even more disturbing by the grainy footage. It carries all the hallmarks of the opening to a torture video from a 1980s horror movie. Coming after the euphoric bliss of the skydive sequence, in which the senses have been purified, we might imagine Bodhi and Utah, having just experienced such a natural high, parting ways with a truce between them. There might have been an understanding that if Bodhi and his crew were to leave town and never return, becoming "ghosts" as Pappas suggested, then all would be forgotten. However, Bodhi has chosen a far more sinister path and has drawn Utah into an underworld of violence and ugliness.

This disturbing image of Tyler, with Rosie cruelly stroking a knife against her face, jolts both the audience and Utah back into the main narrative of the film. Within the film's context, it makes little sense. The jovial nature of the Ex Presidents does not correspond with the cruelty of this footage, especially given that the last time we encountered grainy video imagery like this, it depicted a bare backside with the words "Thank You" scrawled across the cheeks.

This snippet of disturbing footage serves as a harbinger for the scenes of torture depicted in Bigelow's later and controversial film *Zero Dark Thirty* (2012). That film documents the CIA's decade-long pursuit of al-Qaeda leader Osama bin Laden following the attacks on the World Trade Center on September 11, 2001. Its first 25 minutes confront the audience with the methodical brutality inflicted on Ammar al-Baluchi (Reda Kateb), who is shown strung up, shackled, beaten, and waterboarded at a CIA-run black site prison.

The scenes of torture and the film's jingoistic tone brought Bigelow heightened criticism for portraying "enhanced interrogation techniques" as a necessary means of obtaining information from detainees, even though the effectiveness of these techniques was widely disputed in the search for bin Laden. Writing in *The New Yorker*, Jane Mayer observed that the film sidestepped "the political and ethical debate" surrounding the use of torture, suggesting that the procedure in Bigelow's hands "is essentially a police procedural, devoid of moral context."[15] The scenes of al-Baluchi's torture are horrendous and presented with a detachment from both those who instigate the acts and from Bigelow herself. For a brief moment, the scenes play out on a grainy surveillance screen, much as we witness Tyler being bound and gagged in *Point Break*. The scenes in *Zero Dark Thirty* are at least contextually consistent, aligning with the surrounding militaristic narrative. By contrast, the ugly scene of Tyler's capture is contextually out of place within a film that otherwise emphasizes beauty and tranquility.

Minute 86

For the first time during the film, we gain a clearer sense of Bodhi's controlling characteristics. Small flashes of this behavior have appeared throughout the past 85 minutes, with his spiritual calm slipping in short, momentary lapses. Here, we see that Bodhi is willing to unleash an immoral degenerate like Rosie on a person he once considered a friend and, of course, a former lover, in order to protect himself, his comrades, and the continuation of his "endless summer" above all else. Bodhi uses Tyler, as Tim Beasley-Murray states, like "a bargaining chip in the film's violent denouement." Yet Utah also used Tyler to gain access to the surf community. Tyler, therefore, is, as Beasley-Murray concludes, "a play-object, a mere pawn in their schemes."[16]

Though Tyler does not adhere to the typical looks and figure of a female character within an action film, she nonetheless plays a formulaic role within this narrative. According to Lisa Purse in her book *Contemporary Action Cinema*, women, at least within male-led action films, are typically reduced "to the periphery of the space of action, as onlookers or passive victims," while the male figures in the film "bond, share intense physical experiences with each other, and trade looks while showing off their physiques, their weapons and their athletic capacities to each other."[17] Tyler, though ballsy and capable of taking care of herself, has ended up a victim. Her tied-up mouth, legs, and arms leave her helpless and without a voice, though she still manages a grunted "Fuck you" through the gag.

Bodhi hits pause on the portable playback device. Anger boils in Utah, and he lashes out at Bodhi, pushing him against the inside of the van, throttling him, and demanding that he call Rosie to let her go. Bodhi informs him that they are in transit and cannot be contacted. Unless he arrives at a certain destination six hours from now, Rosie will kill Tyler. Bodhi is the key to her survival. He has ensured that only he can survive this trip. Utah lets Bodhi go and slams his fists on the other side of the van. Bodhi catches his breath and states, through a veneer of desperation that he actually "hates violence" and that any other outcome would have been preferred. Bigelow felt that this was an important distinction to make for Bodhi's character. In an interview with Ana Maria Bahiana for *The Guardian*, she noted that "Surfers are not violent people unless they're pushed into a situation. There is certainly a lot of aggression out on the water, but surfing is a singular quest and a personal challenge."[18] Bodhi's position has become one of desperation. He has been pushed into "a situation." Violence is the final option, and he cannot bring himself to perform it, having handed the task to an amoral underling.

Minute 87

Bodhi continues, "Don't you see that's why I need Rosie? I could never do that, man. I could never hold a knife to Tyler's throat." He might not be able to hold the knife himself, but he allows a more depraved individual to do it for him. Bodhi continues discussing his dilemma, bringing up the sadistic image that when "three o'clock comes, he will gut her like a pig and try not to get any on his shoes. I guess that makes us partners." What a terrible image to bestow on Utah, but also on the audience, who have just come out of a blissful skydiving experience. The fact that it comes from Bodhi's mind might indicate the kind of person he really is, or at least the people he associates with who execute such horrors. Utah turns to Bodhi and insists that they are "wasting time." Bodhi exits the van and starts giving instructions to the crew and the pilot. They are hitting the skies once again, but first they have a quick stop to make.

Minute 88

Utah exits the van and slams it in frustration. As the thud resonates on the audio track, it bleeds into the engine roar of the Ex-Presidents' van. The crew are on the road, heading along the highway back into the city. Inside, they kit up in their attire and load weapons for one last bank robbery, now with Utah in tow. Bodhi explains his philosophy for ensuring obedience when managing a frightened crowd of bank patrons.

> **Bodhi:** See it's basic dog psychology, if you scare them and get them peeing down their leg, they submit. Yet, if you project weakness, you draw aggression. That's how people get hurt. You see, fear causes hesitation. And hesitation will cause your worst fears to come true. So, it's simple. You project strength to avoid conflict.

"Peace, through superior firepower," adds Roach with a devilish laugh. This suggests that the Ex-Presidents are more informed students of US presidential history than previously thought and take their get-up a little more seriously. The phrase echoes the "peace through strength" doctrine that has been a feature of US government policy from the post–Second World War era through to the present. Or perhaps the stance has simply bled into the men's subconscious enough that if it worked to suppress smaller nations, it might also seem useful in small-time thievery.

Not wanting a crack-shot FBI agent to disarm the crew mid-robbery, although evidence suggests he would not shoot anyway, Bodhi unloads a shotgun of its shells and hands it to Utah to use as a prop.

Minute 89

Utah looks at the unloaded weapon in his hand and states that "I can't do this." Bodhi informs him that robbing a bank is a "killer rush." He adds that he might, much like surfing and skydiving, even enjoy the action. But Utah is not sold. He tells him to wake up from the illusion that he and his crew are under that he is, after all, an "FBI agent." "FBI" is overly emphasized. Bodhi laughs this off and seems to think taking an agent into a bank robbery will provide an even bigger adrenaline hit. "Why be a servant to the law when you can be its master?" he asks Utah. There is no answer from Utah, but the rest of the crew chime in with their agreement.

Bodhi continues to tell Utah that the 90 seconds of time it takes to rob a bank is a "small price to pay for someone who loves you." He is talking, of course, about Tyler, but for a brief moment, there is some second-guessing as to who he is referring to.

Bodhi passes out the Ex-Presidents masks from a bag. For the first time, we get to see who occupies each mask and persona. He tosses the Jimmy Carter mask to Nathaniel, LBJ goes to Grommet (we now know whose ass it was on the surveillance screen), and the Richard Nixon mask to Roach. This leaves, as we have always suspected, the Ronald Reagan mask for Bodhi to sport.

Minute 90

Bodhi empties out the bag. There is no Gerald Ford mask for Utah. Bodhi slips on his mask. Roach, now with his Nixon mask firmly on, throws his hands up into the iconic double peace sign and proclaims in a Nixonesque grunt, "I'm Ready."

A tense musical flourish kicks in on the soundtrack, as the van pulls up along a busy city street. Bodhi cocks his gun and turns to Utah and instructs him that it is time to "Rock and roll." A grotesque tongue swirls in and out of the mask's mouth hole in a relishing manner.

Bodhi bursts through the back doors of the van and the gang charges inside the bank. We follow the gang into the bank as if we are also a part of the crew. We are watching the events play out from the perspective of Utah as he reluctantly joins them. Inside, the Ex-Presidents maneuver around the room in much the same manner as we saw way back in Minute 7 and 8. In fact, it is hard to believe we have not seen them in action for a vast majority of the film. The camera flies between each member as they rough up the patrons and staff and inflict some of the "basic dog psychology" on them. We find one whimpering patron staring straight into the barrel of the camera's eye. Without the mask, the bank patron maybe feels he can appeal to the human being. Utah instead shouts in his face to get "on the floor, asshole."

Minute 91

Bodhi leans into the frame and points to two surveillance cameras that are recording the whole thing. "Gonna be a little hard to play FBI now," teases Bodhi. This is an interesting comment. Utah has been "playing" an FBI agent for a while now. As he has become more attuned to the surfer lifestyle, he has let his FBI duties and instincts slip.

Utah insists that they should get the money and leave. Bodhi's eyes, disembodied by the mask, for a brief few seconds linger on Utah. Bodhi then jumps on the bank counter and delivers some similar remarks to what he made during that first robbery. He introduces the gang and states that all that is needed is a few moments of everyone's time and it will all be over. Except Bodhi throws a curveball. He turns to Roach/Nixon who is emptying a cash drawer and orders him to "go to the vault." Roach protests this, noticeably dropping the Nixonesque speech. Bodhi's demand has made him slip out of character. This is uncharted territory for them. Roach and Grommet/LBJ pull a female bank worker and the bank's manager out from the captive patrons and proceed to the vault.

Minute 92

Roach directs his gun toward the worker as she fumbles to unlock the security gate. He does not necessarily make matters calmer for the worker as he hurls threats at her to hurry things along. Finally, the vault is open, and Roach and Grommet enter and fill a bag with cash. Back in the main area, Nathaniel/Carter and Bodhi are quietly controlling the room. Utah calls out Bodhi for going for the vault and breaking his own rules. Even though the mask covers his entire face, there appears an obvious sense of panic in Bodhi's usual confidence. The permanent smile and bright white of Reagan's teeth now resemble a pained grimace. His under-the-breath utterance of "It's fine. It's fine. It's great," does not offer reassurance for himself, his comrades, nor the scared bank patrons. He is showing fear and hesitation. Utah walks among the bank patrons who are all face down on the floor. The camera swings down toward a plainclothes off-duty police officer who is among the captives. He whispers to the security guard and shows him his gun that is attached to his belt and asks if he has one concealed. The security guard does not want any trouble and tries to convince the police officer to back down and let the robbery take place.

Minute 93

"When I make a move, you back me up," demands the police officer to the security guard. The guard begs him not to pull out his gun. Roach and Grommet finish in the vault. The police officer slowly retrieves his gun from his belt and stands to direct a bullet toward Bodhi. Utah identifies himself as an FBI agent, but the police officer is already firing. He lands two shots in Utah's chest, which is thankfully protected with a bulletproof vest. Nathaniel fires his shotgun at the police officer and lands a bullet in his upper arm. The guard jumps into action and tries to take out Nathaniel as he rolls across the floor. Roach leaps over the desk and places several bullets in the guard's back. The officer swings around and fires at Roach and Grommet, downing both of them.

A white glove appears over the desk, and the deformed mask of Reagan slowly emerges. Bodhi removes the mask. He looks shocked at the violence that is evident in the room.

Minute 94

The police officer sees Bodhi rise and tries to rearm his gun. Bodhi takes aim and puts a bullet right into the chest of the police officer. His face shows the realization of taking another life. He is shocked by his actions. In this, he shares similar feelings to Utah, who also could not process killing another person. Bodhi's own ego has gotten him into this situation. We have not heard this much gunfire and noise since the raid on the surf punks' house many minutes ago. The shots are deafening.

Utah is wounded by the force of the bullets. He checks himself for injury. His vest saved him. Nathaniel keeps his gun locked on the rest of the patrons. A quietness descends on the room. Bodhi's calm slips as he jumps off the desk and screams, "Nobody fuckin' move!" His face is twisted in rage. He moves toward Grommet, who is lying on the floor bleeding badly. His blood-splattered LBJ mask is still covering his face. He is gravely injured. Blood pours down his front. Bodhi attempts to pick Grommet up off the floor and move him out of the bank.

He affectionately calls him "little brother" a few times as they proceed to the exit.

At no point has it been disclosed that Bodhi and Grommet are siblings, and a quick search of the internet does not confirm or deny the relationship. The only major source is Bojesse Christopher's biography on IMDb, which states that he played the "reckless younger brother of Patrick Swayze" in the film. If Grommet is Bodhi's real brother, this would reveal an even more irresponsible side to Bodhi's persona. Not only has he endangered his friends, but a young and naive member of his own family has been swept up into the carnage. Of course, "little brother" could also be a term of endearment for the group's youngest and most innocent-seeming member.

But then Grommet, realizing he is about to die, holds himself closer to Bodhi's body and whimpers. He passes away in Bodhi's arms, and we see genuine grief wash over Bodhi's face. Dedicating a full ten seconds to reveling in this traumatic loss would seem excessive unless Grommet was his beloved younger brother.

Minute 95

The robbery has disintegrated into a travesty, all because Bodhi saw an opportunity to go for the bank vault and deviate from the well-rehearsed routine of previous robberies. Not only has Grommet been killed, but Nathaniel is furious at Bodhi. He screams, still behind the mask of Carter, "Are you out of your fuckin' mind? Did you get what you wanted?" Roach interjects, "Come on, you can't take him with. Let's go!" The realization hits that his actions have shaken the crew's allegiance to him. He gets up, leaving Grommet's bloody body behind. He sheepishly walks past Utah, who stares him down with a look that reads "I told you so, bro." Bodhi cannot look at Utah directly. The "play without consequences," as Beasley-Murray notes that the Ex-Presidents have engaged in for the past three years has "turned deadly serious."[19] Before he leaves, Bodhi turns and strikes Utah square in the face, knocking him down to the floor. We return to Utah's point of view as he watches the crew hightail it out of the bank. The shot slowly blurs and fades out as Utah loses consciousness.

Consciousness restored. We are back in the bank, which is now teeming with FBI agents, police teams, ambulance crews, forensics, a coroner, and a TV camera operator. Harp bursts in and immediately orders the cameras out of the crime scene. As we pan through the bank, we hear Agent Alvarez reading Miranda rights to someone. When we settle on him, it is Utah who is being arrested. Alvarez cuffs Utah's hands behind his back. He makes no acknowledgment of the situation. He does not respond to Alvarez's verbal insults, nor does he interact with the first responder who is cleaning the cuts to his face. He stares ahead as if in a trance.

It is hard to understand what is going through his head at this point. Is he determined to find Bodhi and apprehend him? Has he forgotten that Rosie still has Tyler held captive with instructions to kill her? Either way, he is not making his case to be released and return to the rescue mission.

Minute 96

The arrival of Pappas breaks Utah out of his daydream. He demands that Utah be uncuffed, but Harp comes over and insists the cuffs remain on. "Your partner's an accessory to murder. You understand that, Pappas?" Harp then directs his wrath toward Utah. "There are three dead people. One of 'em's a police officer, huh?" He then spins Utah around to show him the dead body of the police officer. Utah demands that Harp take his hands off him. Pappas pushes Harp out of the frame and the two have a confrontation that has been long coming. Pappas asks that he be the one to ride Utah to jail. Harp agrees. "Yeah, sure, Angelo. Why not?" "That's why I put you two screw-ups together to begin with. You deserve each other, don't you? It's like the blind leading the blind with you." This triggers Pappas into a response: "Harp, I wanna tell you something. I was in this Bureau when you were still popping zits on your funny face and jackin' off to the lingerie section of the Sears catalog." He then asks Harp what he thinks the biggest lesson of working at the FBI has been all these years.

Minute 97

Pappas delivers a swift and much-deserved punch to Harp's jaw in front of all the other onlookers. He is knocked out cold before he hits the floor. Pappas then gives him the answer to his question, "Respect for my elders. Plain and simple." He then grabs Utah, and they exit the bank.

I am at a strange point in the film. On the streaming service where I have been viewing the film over the past several weeks, I can watch the progress bar move. This is a vital part of watching the film in this minute-by-minute method. I need to ensure I am clocking each minute at the exact moment. However, when I look at the bar, I see that the end of the film is still 25 minutes away, and for the last several days the progress bar has seemed locked and unmoving in this latter part of the film. I check the file data in which I am writing this manuscript. I officially started writing this project on June 2, 2025. It is now late July. I have been watching *Point Break* in this piecemeal and now seemingly unnatural way for eight weeks, and I am still probably two or three weeks away from reaching the end. This is causing me some distress.

All I want to do at this moment is watch the film in its entirety as it was intended. Especially these last 30 minutes or so, which seem so strange and out of place in comparison to the rest of the film. Since the skydiving euphoria of Minute 80–3, the film appears to have taken a strange turn. The lives of the main characters have shifted into a dark funk, which is, of course, true. Everything has been thrown into the air in a discombobulated mix, and now we watch to see what, or who, will land on their feet victorious. All of this would come together in minutes if the film were playing as normal. The stop-start nature of writing means that, for me, the gratification of finishing the film is continually delayed.

I am not alone in thinking that after the skydiving sequence, the film, while still highly enjoyable (in an ordinary screening), becomes a little drawn out. Sean Redmond notes that this stretch of the film feels like a "deliberate form of cinematic excess—an extra turn of the rollercoaster that you weren't expecting, or hadn't paid for."[20] That perception feels more accurate when the film plays out in this slow minute-by-minute format. While certainly allowing the Utah and Bodhi relationship to develop and give the cat-and-mouse chase more screen time, there have been numerous off-ramps for a potential ending to *Point Break* that could have been taken. Redmond continues that the relentlessly stretched-out ending is a conscious decision by Bigelow to "show a number of each more stunning action (body) sequences" and to offer an "extra forty minutes at the expense of the studio system and its (sometimes) reductive template for the action film."[21] In other words, we have another subversion of the typical action genre from Bigelow. We might expect a seamless confrontation between Utah and Bodhi, but it does not happen. We are made to wait for whatever conclusion arrives.

Utah and Pappas drive in silence until Utah informs him that Bodhi and the crew are heading to Santa Monica Airport. Pappas smiles and unlocks Utah's cuffs. He hits the car's accelerator.

They arrive at the airport. A gorgeous wide shot shows their car rolling along the runway toward the camera. A small engine plane is barreling down the runway opposite them and taking off to the left of the screen, while a row of parked planes flanks the right side. A high-rise building lingers in the distance, looking like a hovering spaceship in the shimmering heat. Pappas exits the vehicle and scurries off between the taxied planes. We cut to a wing and a roaring engine. Bodhi and Nathaniel are seen loading up the cargo hold and getting ready for departure.

Minute 98

Bodhi and Nathaniel hear Utah before they see him. The screeching tires indicate trouble is coming. Utah pulls up in front of the plane. The air is shimmering and rippling with the heat from the plane engines and the day's scorching temperatures. Utah gets out of the car and offers up a spin of his body with his arms up in the air, indicating he is unarmed. He even lifts his shirt to reveal his midriff. "But you're not alone," guesses Bodhi correctly as Nathaniel cocks a concealed shotgun. Utah tells the two men that a gun is on them. This information does not seem to faze Bodhi at all. He chortles to himself and continues to load the plane.

We cut to Pappas, who has positioned himself unseen by the fueling pumps outside the main hangar. He directs his gun toward Bodhi.

Back on the runway, Utah asks where Tyler is. Bodhi will not reveal that information and allow his insurance policy to expire. This prompts Utah to suggest that the "ride is over" for him and what remains of the gang. People have died because of his actions. "Oh, no, no. I say when it's over," responds Bodhi coldly. With Nathaniel standing behind and to the side of Bodhi with a concealed shotgun, there is a temptation from the audience's perspective to believe that he might be the one to shoot Bodhi and end the nightmare. Sure, he would be arrested, but a deal could be made with the FBI for a leaner sentence, and Bodhi would be incapacitated.

Minute 99

Utah delivers the news that the man they shot in the bank was an off-duty police officer. They will be picked up wherever they land. The engine on the plane suddenly winds down, and the pilot attempts to exit. Nathaniel demands that he return to the cockpit.

We then see Roach exit the hangar from behind Pappas. He digs into his bag and retrieves his shotgun.

Back on the tarmac, Utah tries to talk Bodhi down. "Look, you got a death wish. You wanna ride to glory? Fine! But don't take Tyler with you," he pleads to Bodhi. "Tell me where she is then I walk away."

Bodhi states that "that is beautiful, Johnny." There is optimism that seeing Utah's noble sentiment is an off-ramp for himself to deescalate the situation. However, the moment is interrupted by Roach cocking his gun and firing it at Pappas. His bullet misses, and Pappas spins and plants two bullets in Roach's chest and stomach. He is unprotected by a vest this time. Nathaniel marches over to Pappas, while Utah attempts to apprehend Bodhi. Pappas lands a bullet in Nathaniel's chest, and he falls to the ground.

Minute 100

Pappas takes aim at Bodhi, but Utah jumps in the way, imploring him not to fire. Bodhi is his only connection to ensuring that Tyler is freed. Utah wants no harm to come to him. As Pappas stands up, a gravely injured Roach pulls his shotgun toward himself and fires twice at Pappas. He hits the floor. Utah screams a prolonged "No." I quickly double back on the progress bar to confirm how long the "No" lingers. A full three seconds of the word is stretched out as Utah sprints toward the injured Pappas, and Bodhi heads over toward the injured Nathaniel. Utah pushes Pappas onto his back, and he mutters that he "doesn't have much time." In the background of the shot, we see Bodhi move from the lifeless Nathaniel and pass Utah and Pappas to check on Roach's condition. Pappas dies in Utah's arms.

Minute 101

The camera sidetracks along with Bodhi and the injured Roach as they rush past the grieving Utah toward the plane. The pilot exits the side hatch and, after witnessing all the commotion, states that he is "not flying you guys to San Felipe." A bleeding Roach orders him to get back on the plane. With the destination revealed aloud, Bodhi commands Utah off the ground and into the plane. "We are gonna ride this all the way, Johnny. You and me," he says. Utah, with a loaded shotgun and a snarling Bodhi in his face, reluctantly moves toward the plane. Sirens begin to wail from the distance. Bodhi pushes Utah into the side hatch and turns to assess the damage. A second comrade has fallen. He grunts as if to hold back a sudden burst of tears and throws the rest of the baggage into the plane. The sirens increase, but the plane is already moving through the thick heat haze and charging up the runway.

Minute 102

A full 15 seconds is devoted to the plane leaving the runway and ascending into the sky. As its wing leaves the frame, we cut to the shadow of the plane flying low over an expanse of shrublands and mountains. Inside the jet, Bodhi radios to Rosie using the call name of "Air Force One." Even after all that has transpired, Bodhi is holding on to the Ex-Presidents moniker and its meaning. There is no response. The pilot calls back to those in the cabin, asking if he can land the plane. Bodhi instructs him to raise the altitude to 4,000 feet. Roach, who is severely injured and bleeding out, thinks that at that altitude they will be picked up by radar. Bodhi needs the plane to reach that height in order to skydive down to the rendezvous destination below. Bodhi helps Roach get his parachute rig on, but Roach comments that he is feeling very cold.

Minute 103

It takes Bodhi almost 20 seconds of carefully wrestling with Roach's injured body to get his coat and parachute rig on. The injuries sustained are causing Roach's body to seize up in pain. When Bodhi asks Utah to hand him a bag of money that Roach will fly down with him, Utah explains to Roach that the reason he is cold is because "all the blood is running out of your body. You're going to be dead soon. I hope it was worth it." Bodhi tells him this is not true, but he knows he is lying to Roach.

Minute 104

Bodhi suits up in his own parachute and places a radio call to Rosie once again. Rosie responds this time. He has Tyler. They are safe. Utah implores Bodhi to give the order to release her. "You got what you wanted. What if your chute fails? Cancel the order!" he pleads. Bodhi contemplates, but he tosses the radio aside and is unwilling. At this point, I must wonder if Bodhi is being hit by a creeping sense of jealousy that Utah is placing Tyler's welfare above his own. Bodhi seems genuinely hurt by the insistence of Utah to let Tyler go, knowing that if she were safe, his pursuit would be called off. Bodhi guides Roach to the side hatch.

Minute 105

Roach signs off with, "I'll see you in hell, Johnny." He laughs as he slips out of the hatch and toward the ground below. Bodhi prepares for his jump. He signals to Utah, "I know it's hard for you, Johnny. I know you want me so bad; it's like acid in your mouth. But not this time." He places his skydiving goggles over his eyes. Oddly, he tosses the gun onto the blankets Roach was resting on. Is this an invitation for Utah to continue the chase? We cut back to Bodhi; his face whipped by the wind. He signs off with, "Adios, amigo," and body-flips out of the plane.

There is no trickery here. This is Swayze falling out of the plane. It is well documented that while preparing and shooting for the film, he became an avid skydiver, telling Bobbie Wygant during a presser, and somewhat echoing his character that it was "truly one of the most beautiful experiences you'll ever feel in your life. More of a sense of aliveness than I've ever felt."[22]

The camera's eye lingers on Bodhi from the edge of the plane as he becomes an ever-decreasing smudge on the lens. Utah is deeply frustrated. He punches the inside of the cabin repeatedly. Then he grabs the discarded gun, aims his body toward the side hatch, and dives after Bodhi with a scream of, "Fucker!" Sam Raimer notes that this reckless action by Utah is an opportunity for him to "hold Bodhi one last time."[23]

He has no chute, no protective clothing or eyewear, and he has only ever skydived once before. All the elements are stacked against his chances of catching up to Bodhi. His decision to leap from the plane is a desperate, instinctual action. It is also incredibly dumb and potentially suicidal. In his desire for Bodhi, rational thought has abandoned him. It is, as Barry Keith Grant notes, a "hysterical visualization of the repressed homoerotic subtext"[24] in the film's representation of Utah and Bodhi's relationship.

Utah free-falls into view of an expansive brown desert landscape, the insect-like specks of Bodhi and Roach falling in the far distance. He moves his body with the air currents, following Bodhi's downward trajectory.

Minute 106

Unlike the beautiful and carefree skydiving sequences witnessed earlier in the film, this time the fall seems fraught with tension. A repeated synth note, with an added splash of cymbal on the soundtrack, heightens the sense of anxiety. We cut back and forth between the unaware Bodhi, freefalling in relative peace, and Utah, who flails in the air with less grace, the wind whipping at his face. We see Utah descend toward Bodhi as if he were Superman. In the wide shot, he guides himself over the top of Bodhi's body and hovers above him for a few moments. He eventually reaches out and grabs Bodhi mid-flight. Much like in Minute 83, when the two men fall toward the Earth and challenge each other to be the first to pull the parachute cord, here, as they fall together in each other's arms, Utah demands that he pull the cord. Bodhi counters that he should be the one to do it. But Utah has a problem. One hand holds firmly to Bodhi's body while the other points a gun at the temple of his head. He cannot let go of Bodhi, and the only other option is to drop the gun and pull the cord. Bodhi knows this, and he also knows that Utah will not shoot him at point-blank range. He knows this because he saw Utah fail to take him out when he had a chance back in Minute 70. He also knows that the sight of blood and gunfire makes Utah squeamish. Bodhi understands that Utah's desire is to take him alive.

Minute 107

"Six seconds. We're gonna be meat waffles!" Bodhi screams.

The ground races toward them. Utah yells at Bodhi, "Pull it! Pull it!"

He tosses the gun and reaches for the parachute cord. They are well below the safe distance from the ground, so the chute's sudden rise does not allow for a graceful landing. Both of them smash onto the desert floor with a thud, sending up a cloud of dust around them.

We cut to a beautifully framed shot of a parachute billowing over a flat desert plain. A body is attached to the cords. Roach is dead. The bags of money he carried down on his descent have split open, and hundreds of notes flutter through the air.

Bodhi and Utah's bodies are wrapped closely together in the parachute sheet. They emerge, and Utah says, "Jesus Christ, Bodhi." They could have just fallen from the sky, or they could have just emerged from a passionate tryst. Either way, the same thirst, passion, and adrenaline have been spent.

Minute 108

Bodhi untangles himself from the chute. "Goddamn, you are one radical son of a bitch," he says to Utah. The two men untether themselves from each other. Both are physically spent.

A car drives toward them through the hot, dusty desert. It is Bodhi's ride. "I'm outta here, Johnny." Utah attempts to get up and leap after Bodhi, but his body is still tangled in the parachute. His knee is also ruptured from the hard landing. Bodhi backs away without much fear. He teases Utah. "Too bad. Looks like this time you won't be getting your man." Utah grunts and groans in frustration. Bodhi admits to Utah that they both lose this game. Utah will not apprehend him. Bodhi has lost all his comrades, and most of the money stolen from the last heist is being whipped across the desert.

Minute 109

But Utah does get a consolation prize of sorts. As Bodhi approaches the vehicle, he shouts at Rosie to let Tyler go. She jumps from the jeep, dressed only in her underwear. She runs toward Utah, collapses in his arms, and the two embrace. There is a sense of relief, but when Tyler attempts to tell Johnny that she loves him, he places his finger over her mouth, much like Tyler did to him in Minute 73, and asks her to tell him how she feels "some other time." Raimer notes that throughout this scene, "Utah has a queer expression on his face, seemingly on the verge of both ecstasy and tears."[25] Of course, there is the physical knee pain he is experiencing from such a rough landing, and the relief that he has saved Tyler from being brutally murdered by Rosie. But he also refuses to "emotionally engage with Tyler," and maintains a "fixed gaze on Bodhi" as he drives away. Similar to Minute 24, when Utah first spotted Bodhi riding the crest of a wave and was instantly besotted, Tyler is again placed between Utah and the fleeing Bodhi, and he cannot take his eyes off him.

Minute 110

But Bodhi cannot leave without saying another goodbye and is compelled to take another dig at Utah's impotence in being unable to apprehend him. "Yo, Johnny!" he shouts. "I'll see you in the next life." While maintaining his tight hold on Tyler, Utah is preoccupied with watching Bodhi and Rosie drive away. Perhaps Utah believes it should be him in the driver's seat with Bodhi by his side. The jeep stops by the body of Roach, and Bodhi jumps out to retrieve the bag containing the rest of the stolen money. They have enough cash to keep on the move for several years. We hear Bodhi say that they should not leave Roach's body behind and that he should be buried in the desert. But Rosie insists there is no time, and they haul the bag into the truck and drive away.

The wind picks up, and a large wall of sand engulfs Utah and Tyler. The camera's eye moves from them and rises above the drifting sand to see the vehicle trailing away into the distance. A line of kicked-up sand snakes behind it—a line that Utah will undoubtedly follow.

We could have had a satisfactory ending of the film happen right here. Utah is reunited with Tyler; the good guy got the girl back. Bodhi, though he got away this time, is left with barely anything for his troubles. His friends, except the delinquent Rosie, are all dead. He will never be able to return to the sweet surf spots of Malibu again for fear of arrest. In fact, for the death of the police officer and the robbery of the bank's safe, the warrant will stretch across the country, if not the entire globe. He will be on the FBI's most wanted fugitives list. The credits could begin to roll right here as the jeep disappears into the distance. The hint of a globe-spanning sequel could easily be implied. Yet *Point Break* offers no such clean exit. Instead, we hear the audio chatter of a radio host, and the patter of heavy rain bleeds over the images of the desert.

Minute 111

The dry desert heat crossfades over a windshield being bombarded by rain. The radio host, with a noticeable Australian accent, warns listeners that the worst storm in Australia's history is about to impact the coastal regions. Through the blurring windshield, we can just make out that the driver is Utah. He looks less like a rookie agent and far more seasoned and grizzled. His hair is longer, and he sips from a can of something. A beer, maybe? He drives through the small town of Torquay in the Surf Coast Shire of Victoria, Australia. The rain is relentless. The radio host mentions that the storm will hit Bells Beach and that residents should evacuate the area. We are swept back to Minute 42, when Bodhi explains to his comrades around the campfire that a once-in-a-lifetime storm will impact this region. Utah made a mental note of Bodhi's death-wish mentality back then. He knows Bodhi will want to surf this break.

Utah parks his truck and exits. He begins to walk down toward the shoreline. These last moments mirror the very first minutes of the film, when Utah expertly shot at paper targets in the rain-drenched practice arena. I go back to those opening minutes on the progress bar and pause on an image of Utah in the rain. In those early moments, he looks youthful, eager to please, and unbothered by the downpour. His clothes fit tightly across his fit physique, and his skin and hair are immaculate. The smile is easygoing and charming. The Utah who exits the rundown truck in these late minutes looks bedraggled, burned out, and exhausted. His dirty denim jeans and jacket combination (a Canadian Tuxedo, if you will) hangs from his wire-thin frame. His long hair looks unwashed and unkempt. The three- to four-day stubble on his face makes him appear older. He resembles Bodhi's more rugged, lived-in manner. He now walks with an unconfident hunch and is clearly bothered by the force of the torrential downpour. He has brought the weather from those first moments with him to rain on Bodhi's parade.

Minute 112

A group of surfers pass him as they leave the beach. When Utah asks about the conditions, one of them motions that the surf is "death on a stick out there, mate." He hurries down the wooden steps that cling to the rock face of Bells Beach. It should be noted, however, that the actual filming location is Indian Beach in Ecola State Park, Oregon.

It might be surprising to learn that Bells Beach is not as sun-drenched and baked as we might expect from seeing scorched Australian landscapes on film and television. Journalist Chas Smith, reflecting on his own experiences surfing Bells Beach, comments that

> when most people think of a surf town, they think of a place that is warm, palm-fringed, laid-back and perpetually sunbathed. And, yet, one of the most iconic surf towns on earth is none of the above. In fact, it actually challenges Detroit, Cleveland and England's Manchester for sheer blue-collar grit. It's a place where clouds hover low most days, bitter cold winds pierce in the winter, and hard-working men and women rise early and head off to factory jobs.[26]

In this case, the rainy and overcast locale of the Pacific Northwest, standing in for Bells Beach, is appropriate.

Utah joins a group of onlookers watching the storm approach and witnesses the building surf. The ocean creates a series of dark, majestic mountains of waves that swirl and smash against each other with frightening force. The dark gray and blue hues make it appear like a moving portrait of the ocean. The light blues and sun-kissed oranges of the Malibu waves seen in earlier scenes have been replaced by a stark, foreboding seascape. The true nature of the ocean.

Utah looks out across the beach. Most people are scurrying from the rain, moving in a hurry. He spots a lone male figure standing at the shore's edge, looking out toward the ocean.

He casually walks across the quickly emptying beach. As he approaches the figure, he takes the Reagan mask out of his jacket pocket and tosses it in front of the lone man. When the mask hits the shoreline, the camera passes in front of the figure, revealing Bodhi. Unlike Utah, Bodhi looks healthier. His bleached-blonde mullet is gone and has been replaced with hair that is trimmed and neatly parted to the side. Bodhi now resembles the "surfing lawyer" style of Utah.

The Reagan mask laps at Bodhi's feet. His past washes up on the shore to haunt him. "Lose something, brah?" Utah asks.

Minute 113

There appears to be little surprise from Bodhi that Utah traveled the world to track him down. As he circles Bodhi, Utah reveals, "I've been to every city in Mexico. Came across an unclaimed piece of meat in Baja. Turned out to be Rosie. Found a passport of yours in Sumatra. Missed you by about a week in Fiji." The two men look longingly toward the towering waves. "I knew you wouldn't miss the fifty-year storm, Bodhi."

Utah lays out the sequel to *Point Break* that was never filmed: a globetrotting cat-and-mouse chase through breathtaking locations, heart-pumping near misses, and a series of extreme sport action scenes even more exhilarating than what we have witnessed here. Instead, that pursuit is left as background noise, as the film moves toward a damp finale in this dimly lit, gray, rain-drenched locale.

Reeves, speaking with WFAA Channel 8 in Dallas as *Point Break* was premiering, joked with the interviewer about a series of films following the exploits of Johnny Utah, FBI agent and surfer. That series never materialized, although we eventually did get Reeves as another ass-kicking John in *John Wick* and its sequels.[27] The enthusiasm was there for a sequel, and the success of the film at the box office warranted one, but it never occurred, and maybe that is a fortunate thing. Too many action films are tainted by diminishing sequel returns; just ask Sylvester Stallone (*Rocky*, *Rambo*) and Willis (*Die Hard*). Arnold Schwarzenegger knew this as well, and apart from the *Terminator* franchise, he stayed away from sequels to the many action films he led, even though some, like *Commando* and *Raw Deal* (1986), seemed to call for it.

We watch as a high, ferocious wave collapses in on itself. The sound is deafening. Utah cuts to the chase, informing Bodhi, "You gotta go down. You crossed the line, people trusted you, and they died." Bodhi casually responds, "Life sure has a sick sense of humor, doesn't it?" He then asks Utah if he still surfs. "Every day," Utah responds matter-of-factly.

Minute 114

Bodhi looks pleased with the answer. Despite all his friends being dead, his life reduced to tatters, and constantly being on the run from the authorities, his legacy and surf philosophy live on in Utah's continued ability and willingness to surf. Utah attempts to lead Bodhi away. "It's time to go. You know you gotta go back with me." Bodhi laughs, as if to say, "The hell I am." It was never going to be that easy. The two men fight and tumble into the shoreline. After much delay within the narrative, the final showdown between protagonist and antagonist—so prevalent in action films—is finally allowed to take place. There is no escape for Bodhi this time. Utah has him cornered.

Minute 115

But just as the fight begins, it is over. Utah gains the advantage, but Bodhi lands a blow to Utah's chest that sends him backward. Bodhi hops on top and delivers a succession of punches to the face. He then pushes Utah under the water and tries to drown him. As Utah loses the will to fight back, Bodhi rises from the shallow water, only to find that Utah has slipped a set of cuffs on him from beneath the waves. A police helicopter appears overhead. "I told them you'd go quietly." Bodhi is beside himself with anger. His actions are now going to be punished. He pleads with Utah, "You know there is no way I can handle a cage, man."

Minute 116

Utah responds, "I don't care. You gotta go down. It's gotta be that way." But Utah does care. Bodhi looks out toward the towering waves. His life has been about reaching this moment, this place in time. He will either be too old, still imprisoned, or not alive to see the next fifty-year storm. However, as discussed previously, the prevalence of these so-called "once-in-a-lifetime" storms means Bodhi might have more opportunity than he believes. But, as it stands, Utah is snatching away a radical dream.

A squad of armed police officers exits the landing helicopter. Bodhi turns to Utah and appeals to the part of him that knows locking him up in a prison cell would be the wrong outcome for such a free-spirited person. He begs, "Look at it, Johnny. Look at it. This is a once-in-a-lifetime opportunity, man. Let me get one wave before you take me. One wave." There is a sense that detaining Bodhi cannot be the resolution the film deserves. Taking him into custody, booking him in jail, and sealing the cage would not be fitting for what we have just witnessed over the past two hours.

Minute 117

Bodhi continues to plead. "My whole life has been about this, Johnny. Come on, compadre." Utah stays silent, his eyes fixed on Bodhi's face, but we can tell he is giving in to the appeal. He looks toward the collapsing walls of water and knows the surf is not survivable. Bodhi will be crushed to death by the sheer weight of it. His death wish is clear. He is not pleading for release so he can be captured later after catching a few waves; he is pleading to be allowed to die in the surf. The "one wave" is all he needs. He knows his life is over, no matter what. The two men linger on each other for a few moments. Utah unlocks the cuffs and hands Bodhi over—"not to the law," as David Greven observes, but "to his own desire for self-immolation within those world-engulfing waves," and to the same "death-drive masochism"[28] that was discussed around the campfire all the way back in Minute 42 and first introduced by Tyler when Utah first laid eyes on Bodhi in the surf in Minute 24. Those minutes now feel like a lifetime ago—both within the context of the film itself and from the perspective of Utah and Bodhi's tumultuous relationship.

Minute 118

Utah then bids Bodhi, "Vata con Dios" (Be with God). It is interesting that Bodhi used a Spanish phrase to solidify his relationship with Utah ("de nada") back in Minute 38, and now Utah uses another to sever it. Bodhi quickly grabs his board and runs out toward the waves. The Australian police arrive on the beach and are livid with Utah for allowing the fugitive to escape. "You let him go!" screams one of the officers. Utah looks into the surf and utters, "No, I didn't." We see Bodhi climb the face of the monstrous waves. A police officer remarks, "We'll get him when he comes back in." Utah may have let Bodhi go in the eyes of the law, but his fate is sealed on the waves. Already leaving the scene, Utah retorts to himself, "He's not coming back." Though Bodhi's body might wash up on the shore after the storm abates, his spirit will be gone.

Minute 119

Bodhi sits atop the gargantuan wave, and as he begins to descend, the curl pushes him off the board and into the wash of the water. The tumbling white water engulfs Bodhi in a fierce froth and mist. Presumably, he is crushed by the weight and rush of the water and sent to the bottom of the ocean.

American artist Raymond Pettibon's painting *No Title (We devoutly hope . . .)* depicts a lone surfer, ghostlike, blended with an enormous, towering wave. Art historian Brian Lukacher comments on the piece that "the uncertainty of survival and the near eradication of the surfer is more urgently felt. The wave lines here are taut and repetitive, forming a constricting web of tendrils around the figure. The surfer disappears within a vertical shaft of torrential rain, as if a violent microclimate has taken shape inside the tightening coil of the sea."[29]

The painting bears a striking similarity to Bodhi's final moments as he falls into the all-encompassing wave, conveying a sense of futility against the ocean's extremes.

As Utah continues his stride along the beachfront, he takes his FBI badge out of his pocket and holds it in his hand, eyeing it for a few seconds. He nonchalantly tosses the badge into the shallows, where it lands with a splash. According to Sean Redmond, he has rejected the rigor of the "political order for, at least implicitly, counter-culture values and lifestyle," while also rejecting the "surveillance culture and the dominant system of law and order."[30] Yet, much like the infatuation Utah felt for Bodhi upon their first meeting, he has been drawn into the mythology of Bodhi's longing to die doing what he loves. He has allowed Bodhi to become a mythic figure, granting him immortality among the surf sages and extreme sports enthusiasts.

Interestingly, the slate-gray clouds begin to clear, with a sliver of blue sky emerging and a beam of sunshine breaking through. Utah, with a grin, walks out of frame. He is content. The scene cuts to black as the song "Nobody Rides for Free" by California glam rock band RATT kicks in while the cast and crew credits roll. The song serves as a fitting finale. Bodhi's ride is over. The price paid is his own life and the lives of everyone in his immediate orbit. It was never a "free ride" after all.

In some respects, the ending of *Point Break* shares similarities with the ending of Don Siegel's *Dirty Harry* (1971), in which San Francisco Inspector Harry Callahan (Clint Eastwood) discards his badge in a river after killing the film's antagonist, Scorpio (Andrew Robinson). While both actions are symbolic, the feelings of frustration and disillusionment with the work of protection and service are experienced by both Callahan and Utah. However, I believe the discarding of the FBI badge shares more in common with the moment in Dennis Hopper's *Easy Rider*, in which the central character, Wyatt, after scoring a big payout from a drug deal in Mexico, throws his Timex watch to the dirt at the beginning of the film. This action is considered a rejection of society's constraints, its rigid measures of time and how to spend it (at work, at school, etc.), and, in some respects, an objection to obsession with ownership and materialism. Wyatt and his companion Billy are now free to roam at their own pace and in their own time, just as Utah is now that he has thrown down the shackles of his own bondage.

A cynical reading of the film's ending might lead one to conclude that Utah's future is in disarray and that all avenues are closed to him. He has ended his career, and the surfing he performs every day may be a solitary and unsatisfying endeavor. Without the spiritual guidance of Bodhi, he is just treading water. Tim Beasley-Murray takes this perspective, stating that the "Utah of the end of the film—unshaven and disheveled—disconsolately gives up playing at all, envious of Bodhi's pointless death, sick of life and its games, an anonymous, badge-less, role-less outcast with a dodgy knee."[31] It is also another neat subversion of the typical action-hero narrative, in which the protagonist has acquired a set of skills and knowledge that will persist into future adventures. Lisa Purse calls this the "narrative of becoming," in which the action hero's "physical and emotional trajectory toward achieving full occupation of the heroic action body"[32] is accomplished. Utah rejects his set of skills and knowledge, his FBI training and field experience that would have propelled him toward further encounters with thieves and crooks, in favor of the lessons he has gained from Bodhi. I like to consider Utah discarding his badge as symbolic of his rejection of the law and order he has served, and instead an embrace of the countercultural lifestyle that surfing offers. His subtle, determined smile to himself as he walks out of frame signals the realization that his life is about to begin outside the constraints of the film's frame.

Utah has both lost himself and found himself, just as Bodhi predicted.

Postscript

One of my apprehensions when I first considered writing a minute-by-minute analysis of *Point Break* was the unintentional side effect of exorcizing the film from my own consciousness. Several years ago, I tackled *Dirty Dancing* (another Patrick Swayze film—what is wrong with me?) in a similar structure to this project. I enjoyed the months-long process of watching and dissecting the film scene by scene, exploring its many layers of class, gender, race, politics, and cultural significance, along with the supplementary reading and research that accompanied it. Yet, once the project was complete, the simple pleasure of watching *Dirty Dancing* had dissolved. Now the film had become a text I had dissected almost to death. I had peered too closely, and the experience of simply watching and enjoying it for the film it is had become tainted. Ten years after that project wrapped, I have yet to return to *Dirty Dancing* in any capacity. Though I still recommend it to anyone willing to listen, for now, at least, I am spent.

Throughout this process, my desire to watch *Point Break* as it was intended became, at some points, overwhelming, and I found myself losing the thread of the minute I was analyzing as the next minute rolled around and the one after that. In some instances, I would unknowingly allow ten riveting minutes of the film to play out before realizing what the task at hand was. Frustratingly, I would have to stop the film and crawl back along the progress bar to return to the minute of direct analysis, knowing that my gratification would have to come later, when the transcript of each minute was processed onto the page. I could then allow myself a full screening of the film without the pauses, the crawl backs, and the repeated viewing of dialogue scenes to ensure I had heard everything correctly.

For example, the foot-chase sequence found in Minutes 68–71 became an impossible task to stop. The whole sequence barely made sense without the preceding and subsequent minutes. Time seemed to move more quickly within this portion of the film; it became unnoticeable, escaping my careful eye. The same could be said for both skydiving scenes. It was hard to pause when the majesty of the moment could flow on and on, immersing me in the film.

Thankfully, my apprehension evaporated. A few weeks after completing what I considered to be the bulk of the manuscript I strapped in for a full screening of *Point Break*. As it had been through all previous screenings prior to this project, the film flowed at a whip-fast pace. All the scenes and sequences rolled around. Familiar? Certainly. Overly so? Possibly. But that familiarity was still riveting. All the usual elements of the film that had thrilled me, made me giggle, and put me in a state of awe were still intact. The surface pleasure of watching the film for simple enjoyment thankfully remained.

This is the beauty of all films: they exist as a medium for communal or solitary entertainment. That is our first question we consider when watching a film at the cinema, on DVD, or on a streaming service. Will we enjoy ourselves? However, scratching the surface of that entertainment layer can reveal much about the filmmakers' intentions and ideology. The small nuances that hover as "reality effects" in a film's miasma come to the foreground and allow for interpretation and revelation. This offers an enlightenment that feeds the very soul.

NOTES

Immersion

1 Broxton, J. (2021). "Point Break—Mark Isham." *Movie Music UK*. https://moviemusicuk.us/2021/08/05/point-break-mark-isham/, accessed August 11, 2025.

2 Ibid.

3 Redmond, S. (2003). "All That Is Male Melts into Air." In *The Cinema of Kathryn Bigelow: Hollywood Transgressor*, eds. Jermyn, D. and Redmond, S. London: Wallflower Press, 106.

4 Giarratana, C. (2002). "The Keanu Effect—Stardom and the Landscape of the Acting Body: Los Angeles/Hollywood as Sight/Site." In *Stars in Our Eyes: The Star Phenomenon in the Contemporary Era*, eds. Ndalianis, A. and Henry, C. Westport: Praeger, 70.

5 Utah Legislature (2003). "H.B. 223: Changing State Song." *Utah State Legislature*. https://le.utah.gov/~2003/bills/static/HB0223.html, accessed August 28, 2025.

6 Grant, B. K. (1996). *Shadows of Doubt: Negotiations of Masculinity in American Genre Films*. Detroit: Wayne State University Press, 186.

7 Beasley-Murray, T. (2025). "Play and Performance, Perfection and Pessimism: A Reassessment of (the Politics of) *Point Break*." *Journal of Popular Film and Television*, 53 (1–2), 48. https://doi.org/10.1080/01956051.2025.2508695.

8 Cambridge University Press (2025). "Harp." *Cambridge English Dictionary*. https://dictionary.cambridge.org/dictionary/english/harp, accessed June 8, 2025.

9 Beasley-Murray, T. (2025). "Play and Performance, Perfection and Pessimism: A Reassessment of (the Politics of) Point Break." *Journal of Popular Film and Television*, 53 (1–2), 48. https://doi.org/10.1080/01956051.2025.2508695.

10 Redmond, S. (2003). "All That Is Male Melts into Air." In *The Cinema of Kathryn Bigelow: Hollywood Transgressor*, eds. Jermyn, D. and Redmond, S. London: Wallflower Press, 114.

11 Ibid., 113.

12 Beasley-Murray, T. (2025). "Play and Performance, Perfection and Pessimism: A Reassessment of (the Politics of) *Point Break*." *Journal of Popular Film and Television*, 53 (1–2), 51. https://doi.org/10.1080/01956051.2025.2508695.

13 Urban Dictionary (2025). "Blue Flamer." *Urban Dictionary*. https://www.urbandictionary.com/define.php?term=blue%20flamer, accessed June 28, 2025.

14 Gerald R. Ford Presidential Library (2025). "Key Speeches and Writings of Gerald R. Ford." https://www.fordlibrarymuseum.gov/the-fords/gerald-r-ford/key-speeches-and-writings-gerald-r-ford, accessed June 5, 2025.

15 Ibid.

16 Beasley-Murray, T. (2025). "Play and Performance, Perfection and Pessimism: A Reassessment of (the Politics of) *Point Break*." *Journal of Popular Film and Television*, 53 (1–2), 49. https://doi.org/10.1080/01956051.2025.2508695.

17 Rath, A. (2013). "I Am Not a Crook: How a Phrase Got a Life of Its Own." *NPR*, November 17. https://www.npr.org/2013/11/17/245830047/i-am-not-a-crook-how-a-phrase-got-a-life-of-its-own, accessed June 16, 2025.

18 Reimer, S. (2019). "'Young, Dumb, and Full of Cum': *Point Break*'s Homoerotic Haze in Five Acts." *The Neutral*, Cinema Studies Institute at the University of Toronto. https://jps.library.utoronto.ca/index.php/theneutral/article/view/36005/27320, accessed August 3, 2025.

19 Ibid.

20 Baudrillard, J. (1995). "Los Angeles by Night." In *West of the West: Imagining California*, eds. Michaels, L., Reid, D., and Scherr, R. Berkeley: University of California Press, 62.

21 Davis, M. (1990). *City of Quartz: Excavating the Future in Los Angeles*. New York: Verso, x.

22 Davis, M. (1998). *Ecology of Fear: Los Angeles and the Imagination of Disaster*. New York: Metropolitan Books, 417.

23 Friedersdorf, C. (2018). "The Battle of Khe Sanh and Its Retellings." *The Atlantic*. https://www.theatlantic.com/politics/archive/2018/01/the-battle-of-khe-sanh-and-its-retellings/551315/, accessed June 17, 2025.

24 Buckwalter, I. (2014). "Revisiting an 'Endless Summer'." *NPR*. https://www.npr.org/2014/07/24/334459717/revisiting-an-endless-summer, accessed August 15, 2025.

25 Ford, N. and Brown, D. (2006). *Surfing and Social Theory: Experience, Embodiment, and Narrative of the Dream Glide*. London: Routledge, 77.

26 Arn, J. (2024). "The Point of 'Point Break.'" *The New Yorker*. https://www.newyorker.com/culture/cultural-comment/the-point-of-point-break, accessed June 5, 2025.

27 Tasker, Y. (1999). "Bigger Than Life." In *Action/Spectacle Cinema: A Sight and Sound Reader*, ed. Arroyo, J. London: British Film Institute, 198.

28 Collins, L. (2012). "100% Pure Adrenaline: Gender and Generic Surface in Point Break." In *Gender Meets Genre in Postwar Cinemas*, ed. Gledhill, C. Champaign: University of Illinois Press, 54.

29 Everett, P. (2004). "Alluvial Deposits." In *Damned If I Do: Stories*. St. Paul: Graywolf Press, 39–59.

30 Redmond, S. (2003). "All That Is Male Melts into Air." In *The Cinema of Kathryn Bigelow: Hollywood Transgressor*, eds. Jermyn, D. and Redmond, S. London: Wallflower Press, 118.

31 Ibid.

32 Kuhns, G. W. (1963). *On Surfing*. Vermont: Charles E. Tuttle Company, 120.

33 Lamb, A. (2020). "Point Break and the Subversion of Surfing." *A Fistful of Film*. https://afistfuloffilm.movie.blog/2020/03/21/point-break-1991-and-the-subversion-of-surfing/, accessed August 4, 2025.

34 National Transportation Safety Board (1984). "CAROL Query: January 1984." https://data.ntsb.gov/carol-main-public/query-builder?month=1&year=1984, accessed June 6, 2025.

35 National Interagency Fire Center (1983–2024). "Wildfires and Acres." https://www.nifc.gov/fire-information/statistics/wildfires, accessed June 9, 2025.

36 Salguero, P. (2022). "What Is a Bodhisattva? A Scholar of Buddhism Explains." *The Conversation*. https://theconversation.com/what-is-a-bodhisattva-a-scholar-of-buddhism-explains-189366, accessed June 13, 2025.

37 Reimer, S. (2019). "'Young, Dumb, and Full of Cum': Point Break's Homoerotic Haze in Five Acts." *The Neutral*, Cinema Studies Institute at the University of Toronto. https://jps.library.utoronto.ca/index.php/theneutral/article/view/36005/27320, accessed August 3, 2025.

38 Kuhns, G. W. (1963). *On Surfing*. Vermont: Charles E. Tuttle Company, 88–9.

39 Malin, B. J. (2005). *American Masculinity Under Clinton: Popular Media and the Nineties*. New York: Peter Lang Publishing, 30.

40 Ford, N. and Brown, D. (2006). *Surfing and Social Theory: Experience, Embodiment, and Narrative of the Dream Glide*. London: Routledge, 145.

41 Barscay, K. (2010). "Kathryn Bigelow's Gen(d)re." *Cinephile*. https://cinephile.ca/archives/volume-4-post-genre/essay-1, accessed August 1, 2025.

42 Smith, G. (2016). "Momentum and Design: Kathryn Bigelow Interviewed." In *Kathryn Bigelow: Interviews*, ed. Keough, P. Jackson: University of Mississippi Press, 80.

43 Pettibon, B. and Lukacher, B. (2022). *Point Break: Raymond Pettibon, Surfers and Waves*. New York: David Zwirner Books, 9.

44 Hill, L. (1996). *Easy Rider*. London: British Film Institute, 44.

45 Stranger, M. (2011). *Surfing Life: Surface, Substructure and the Commodification of the Sublime*. London: Routledge, 25.

46 Reimer, S. (2019). "'Young, Dumb, and Full of Cum': Point Break's Homoerotic Haze in Five Acts." *The Neutral*, Cinema

Studies Institute at the University of Toronto. https://jps.library.utoronto.ca/index.php/theneutral/article/view/36005/27320, accessed August 3, 2025.

47 Tasker, Y. (1993). *Spectacular Bodies: Gender, Genre and the Action Cinema*. London: Routledge, 164.

48 Ford, N. and Brown, D. (2006). *Surfing and Social Theory: Experience, Embodiment, and Narrative of the Dream Glide*. London: Routledge, 107.

49 Pinto, L. M. (2020). "The Best Quotes by Mark Foo." *Surfer Today*. https://www.surfertoday.com/surfing/the-best-quotes-by-mark-foo, accessed July 26, 2025.

50 Smith, C. (2020). "Bells Beach." In *Lonely Planet Epic Surf Breaks of the World: Explore the Planet's Most Thrilling Waves*. Victoria: Lonely Planet Global Limited, 282.

51 Ibid.

52 Kluger, J. (2025). "Why 'Hundred-Year' Weather Events Are Happening More Than Once Every 100 Years." *Time*. https://time.com/7289719/hundred-year-weather-events-happen-more-often/, accessed August 12, 2025.

53 Khalil, S. (2025). "Japan Court Dissolves Controversial 'Moonies' church." *BBC*, March 25. https://www.bbc.com/news/articles/cge1lr7225yo, accessed July 23, 2025.

54 Kuhns, G. W. (1963). *On Surfing*. Vermont: Charles E. Tuttle Company, 15.

55 Fiouzi, A. (2020). "I Once Lived for Danger. Night Surfing Scared Me Straight." *MEL*. https://melmagazine.com/en-us/story/i-once-lived-for-danger-night-surfing-scared-me-straight, accessed June 23, 2025.

56 Redmond, S. (2003). "All That Is Male Melts into Air." In *The Cinema of Kathryn Bigelow: Hollywood Transgressor*, eds. Jermyn, D. and Redmond, S. London: Wallflower Press, 114.

57 James, A. (2017). *Surfing with Sartre: An Aquatic Inquiry into a Life of Meaning*, New York: Doubleday, 46.

58 Johnson, T. (1990). "James Cameron and Kathryn Bigelow." In *Kathryn Bigelow: Interviews*, ed. Keough, P. Jackson: University of Mississippi Press, 59.

59 Interview conducted by Anthony Mason for *CBS News*. https://www.cbsnews.com/video/eddie-vedder-on-the-origin-of-pearl-jam-it-was-heaven/, accessed July 29, 2025.

60 Smith, G. (2016). "Momentum and Design: Kathryn Bigelow Interviewed." In *Kathryn Bigelow: Interviews*, ed. Keough, P. Jackson: University of Mississippi Press, 78.

61 Ibid., 80.

62 Redmond, S. (2003). "All That Is Male Melts into Air." In *The Cinema of Kathryn Bigelow: Hollywood Transgressor*, eds. Jermyn, D. and Redmond, S. London: Wallflower Press, 117.

63 Barscay, K. (2010). "Kathryn Bigelow's Gen(d)re." *Cinephile*. https://cinephile.ca/archives/volume-4-post-genre/essay-1, accessed August 1, 2025.

64 Ibid.

Revelation

1 Lincoln Moter Company (2012). https://web.archive.org/web/20130403124132/http://media.lincoln.com/images/10031/LMC_Briefing_Book.pdf, accessed June 27, 2025.

2 Cannon, L. (2017). "Ronald Reagan: Life Before the Presidency." *Miller Center*. https://millercenter.org/president/reagan/life-before-the-presidency, accessed August 3, 2025.

3 Nerdwriter (Puschak, E). (2024). "The Director Who Revolutionized The POV Shot." *YouTube*. https://www.youtube.com/watch?v=cA7u578i5oc&t=4s, accessed June 30, 2025.

4 Collins, L. (2012). "100% Pure Adrenaline: Gender and Generic Surface in *Point Break*." In *Gender Meets Genre in Postwar Cinemas*, ed. Gledhill, C. Champaign: University of Illinois Press, 62–3.

5 Ibid., 63.

6 Broxton, J. (2021). "Point Break—Mark Isham." *Movie Music UK*. https://moviemusicuk.us/2021/08/05/point-break-mark-isham/, accessed August 11, 2025.

7 Smith, G. (2016). "Momentum and Design: Kathryn Bigelow Interviewed." In *Kathryn Bigelow: Interviews*, ed. Keough, P. Jackson: University of Mississippi Press, 80.

8 Greven, D. (2009). *Manhood in Hollywood from Bush to Bush*. Austin: University of Texas Press, 148.

9 Redmond, S. (2003). "All That Is Male Melts into Air." In *The Cinema of Kathryn Bigelow: Hollywood Transgressor*, eds. Jermyn, D. and Redmond, S. London: Wallflower Press, 120–1.

10 Reimer, S. (2019). "'Young, Dumb, and Full of Cum': Point Break's Homoerotic Haze in Five Acts." *The Neutral*, Cinema Studies Institute at the University of Toronto. https://jps.library.utoronto.ca/index.php/theneutral/article/view/36005/27320, accessed August 4, 2025.

11 Reimer, S. (2019). "'Young, Dumb, and Full of Cum': Point Break's Homoerotic Haze in Five Acts." *The Neutral*, Cinema Studies Institute at the University of Toronto. https://jps.library.utoronto.ca/index.php/theneutral/article/view/36005/27320, accessed 4 August 4, 2025.

12 Collins, L. (2012). "100% Pure Adrenaline: Gender and Generic Surface in *Point Break*." In *Gender Meets Genre in Postwar Cinemas*, ed. Gledhill, C. Champaign: University of Illinois Press, 63.

13 Bobbie Wygant Archive (2021). "Katheryn Bigelow 'Point Break' 6/8/91—Bobbie Wygant Archive." *YouTube*. https://www.youtube.com/watch?v=GlRilrvAXwI, accessed August 9, 2025.

14 Greven, D. (2009). *Manhood in Hollywood from Bush to Bush*. Austin: University of Texas Press, 148.

15 Mayer, J. (2012). "Zero Conscience in 'Zero Dark Thirty'." *The New Yorker*. https://www.newyorker.com/news/news-desk/zero-conscience-in-zero-dark-thirty, accessed August 28, 2025.

16 Beasley-Murray, T. (2025). "Play and Performance, Perfection and Pessimism: A Reassessment of (the Politics of) Point Break." *Journal of Popular Film and Television*, 53 (1–2), 54. https://doi.org/10.1080/01956051.2025.2508695.

17 Purse, L. (2011). *Contemporary Action Cinema*. Edinburgh: Edinburgh University Press, 133.

18 Bahiana, A. M. (2013). "Kathryn Bigelow." In *Kathryn Bigelow: Interviews*, ed. Keough, P. Jackson: University Press of Mississippi, 68.

19 Beasley-Murray, T. (2025). "Play and Performance, Perfection and Pessimism: A Reassessment of (the Politics of) Point Break." *Journal of Popular Film and Television*, 53 (1–2), 54. https://doi.org/10.1080/01956051.2025.2508695.

20 Redmond, S. (2003). "All That Is Male Melts into Air." In *The Cinema of Kathryn Bigelow: Hollywood Transgressor*, eds. Jermyn, D. and Redmond, S. London: Wallflower Press, 123.

21 Ibid., 124.

22 The Bobbie Wygant Archive (2021). "Patrick Swayze 'Point Break' 6/8/91—Bobbie Wygant Archive." *YouTube*. https://www.youtube.com/watch?v=WIdcSc0wPOI&t=2s, accessed September 4, 2025.

23 Reimer, S. (2019). "'Young, Dumb, and Full of Cum': Point Break's Homoerotic Haze in Five Acts." *The Neutral*, Cinema Studies Institute at the University of Toronto. https://jps.library.utoronto.ca/index.php/theneutral/article/view/36005/27320, accessed August 4, 2025.

24 Grant, B. K. (1996). *Shadows of Doubt: Negotiations of Masculinity in American Genre Films*. Detroit: Wayne State University Press, 187.

25 Reimer, S. (2019). "'Young, Dumb, and Full of Cum': Point Break's Homoerotic Haze in Five Acts." *The Neutral*, Cinema Studies Institute at the University of Toronto. https://jps.library.utoronto.ca/index.php/theneutral/article/view/36005/27320, accessed August 3, 2025.

26 Smith, C. (2020). "Bells Beach." In *Lonely Planet Epic Surf Breaks of the World: Explore the Planet's Most Thrilling Waves*. Victoria: Lonely Planet Global Limited, 282.

27 WFAA Dallas (2025). "Keanu Reeves Discusses Playing Johnny Utah in Point Break (1991)." *YouTube*. https://www.youtube.com/watch?v=GDgvPIWBTkc, accessed August 5, 2025.

28 Greven, D. (2009). *Manhood in Hollywood from Bush to Bush*. Austin: University of Texas Press, 149.

29 Pettibon, B. and Lukacher, B. (2022). *Point Break: Raymond Pettibon, Surfers and Waves*. New York: David Zwirner Books, 9.

30 Redmond, S. (2003). "All That Is Male Melts into Air." In *The Cinema of Kathryn Bigelow: Hollywood Transgressor*, eds. Jermyn, D. and Redmond, S. London: Wallflower Press, 108.

31 Beasley-Murray, T. (2025). "Play and Performance, Perfection and Pessimism: A Reassessment of (the Politics of) Point Break." *Journal of Popular Film and Television*, 53 (1–2), 56. https://doi.org/10.1080/01956051.2025.2508695.

32 Purse, L. (2011). *Contemporary Action Cinema*. Edinburgh: Edinburgh University Press, 33.

INDEX